The Tough Kid

New Teacher Kit

**Practical Classroom Management
Survival Strategies for the New Teacher**

Ginger Rhode, Ph.D.
William R. Jenson, Ph.D.
Daniel P. Morgan, Ph.D.

Edited by Mitchell Duval
Cover and layout design by Becky Malone
Illustrated by Tom Oling

ISBN 1-57035-468-5

Printed in the United States of America

Published and Distributed by

SOPRIS
WEST
EDUCATIONAL SERVICES

4093 Specialty Place • Longmont, CO 80504 • (303) 651-2829
www.sopriswest.com

218MAN/1-05/BAN

Dedication

This manual is dedicated to all the "new young lions,"
as our colleague Ken Reavis used to say.

"Our children are our hope for the future,
but we are the hope for theirs."

—Anonymous

Contents

Section 8

Section 9

Section 10

Section 11

Section 12

References

Preface

You are a new teacher, and you are about to begin your career in education. We think starting a career in education is a bit like starting a journey. That is why we use airplane metaphors at the beginning of each section to illustrate the variety of critical junctures that will occur during this important first year. We hope the metaphorical similarities between our air travel journey and your first year as a teacher will make our messages more meaningful and memorable as you read and use this manual.

We also want to make a couple of other important points before you begin this manual, or journey. The information we present in the pages ahead is based on proven, practical, research-based strategies that are used in classrooms where students are successful, both academically and behaviorally. In a sense, this will be a "no frills" flight. This should not deter you from booking with us, however, because the basic menu of research-based options we include in this kit offer you plenty of choices to handle the majority of situations you will encounter during your first year as a teacher.

We also recognize that our approach and the kit we have packaged may possibly be viewed as "cookbookish." Such a label is very ironic since we love to cook, and we view authoring a cookbook as an accomplishment! Cookbooks are indispensable aids for aspiring new cooks who, with experience and practice, will eventually become master chefs who improvise as they create masterpieces.

Another possible comment about this kit may be that what we have packaged is

> *The options we include in this kit offer you plenty of choices to handle the majority of situations you will encounter during your first year as a teacher.*

nothing more than "behavior management in a box." Actually, we take such a comment as a compliment. Most of the essential materials and information you will need to start an effective classroom management system are contained in this kit. Time is your most precious resource as a new teacher. We do not want you searching all over the place for the materials you need, nor do we want you having to make them from scratch.

One other "heads up" before you start reading this manual in earnest. You will meet a rather crotchety, set-in-her-ways, and very opinionated character in the pages ahead. Her name is Mrs. Muttner. She is a bit like the annoying passenger in the seat next to you on a trip who won't stop talking, when all you are trying to do is have a pleasant journey. Mrs. Muttner is on board in this manual's journey as well, but we think we have provided you with some effective countermeasures to the "Muttnerisms" peppered throughout the sections ahead.

Again, you are about to begin your journey. We hope it is a great adventure full of fascinating and memorable experiences. Our goal is to make this trip as enjoyable and successful for you as we can. Best of luck!

Section 1

Anticipating the Trip Ahead:

Why You Should Read This Manual and What It Will Do for You

If you are reading this sentence, you are probably a first-year teacher. You may have just completed your teacher preparation program or are just starting a program that will lead to a teaching license. Perhaps you are returning to teaching after an extended absence or you are someone who works with new teachers. Much has been written about the needs of new teachers and the problems they encounter. We think this manual is unique, because its primary focus is the main challenge faced by new teachers—finding practical solutions for preventing and dealing with the misbehavior of students.

Of course, new teachers run into other problems besides classroom discipline and behavior management. General working conditions, such as class size, availability of curricular materials, and feelings of isolation and lack of support contribute to the challenges faced by new teachers in their first year (Harris & Associates, 1991). These problems have a profound impact on new teachers. It has been estimated that up to 50 percent of all new teachers will leave the profession within the first five years of teaching (Recruiting New Teachers, 2000). In recent years, it has become even more unlikely that a new teacher will become a veteran teacher.

Why do new teachers have difficulties in their first year? Many reasons combine to produce the poor teacher retention that our schools have been experiencing, but a few in particular contribute to the difficulties encountered by many teachers:

- New teachers have a difficult time transferring the theory they have learned to actual practice in the classroom. Some teachers may be very knowledgeable when it comes to elegant educational theories or the social/philosophical foundations of education. Some may be knowledgeable about a variety of curriculum materials and methods. But knowing too much of the wrong information and too little of the relevant information often results in some serious stumbling.

- Many new teachers simply lack the preparation they need prior to entering the profession. Their teacher preparation program may have emphasized campus-based coursework in education. They may have had virtually no meaningful field-based practical experiences in schools. Their preparation may have also emphasized teaching strategies with no firm support in the research literature as to their effectiveness. What some new teachers may have been taught in their preparation programs about behavior management, for example, may be virtually useless with students on a day in and day out basis.

- There are large numbers of individuals teaching in classrooms all over the United States who have had *no* preparation prior to their first year of teaching. These individuals are referred to in a variety of ways: provisional, temporary, unlicensed, unqualified, or transi-

tional teachers. Many are enrolled in Alternative Teacher Preparation programs where they can complete coursework that leads to a full teaching credential in a specific educational area. For the vast majority of these teachers, their lack of preparation underlines the critical need for a great deal of support and guidance in their first year of teaching.

- Many new teachers are often placed in the toughest schools with the toughest kids, and, in these tough schools, there is often a serious shortage of resources available to new teachers. From a lack of good quality curriculum materials to a shortage of basic classroom supplies, new teachers in these settings are often forced into "making do" throughout their entire first-year experience.

- New teachers may be reluctant to seek help or ask questions. They may fear that doing so will be perceived as a sign of weakness or as a sign that they do not know what they are doing. Many would rather struggle alone than reveal themselves to be in need of support and guidance.

- Finally, and inevitably, new teachers often experience a serious reduction in their sense of efficacy, that is, the belief that what they are doing makes a difference. At the beginning of their first year, they may face hurdles they believe can be overcome. Later, these hurdles may turn into huge walls that seem insurmountable. This is likely due to the interaction of all of the difficulties mentioned in this section.

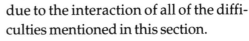

This manual has been designed to address each of these issues. The strategies and techniques presented in this manual are not panaceas, nor are they magical solutions. They are, however, well grounded in theory and research *and* are very practical and easy to use "right out of the box." This manual should help you a lot as you navigate your first year in the classroom.

Organization of This Manual

We have organized this manual into twelve sections. **Section 1** is introductory in nature, telling you a bit about what you can expect from this manual. **Section 2** offers specific suggestions for getting ready for the important first few days of your first year. **Section 3** addresses the classroom rules and procedures that will form the foundation of all of your other teaching activities for the rest of the year. **Section 4** tells you how to use Precision Requests to increase student compliance. **Section 5** describes the use of both positive and undesired consequences and how to combine their use in a classroom What If? Chart. **Section 6** describes how to increase your effectiveness by adding even more positive strategies to your classroom. **Section 7** provides you with additional "beyond the basics" strategies. **Section 8** tells you what to do when what you have already read about in the previous sections doesn't work with your chronic rule breakers. **Section 9** provides strategies for additional special behavior problems. **Section 10** describes classroom accommodations some of your students with special needs might require in order to be successful. **Section 11** provides you with additional ideas you can use to help you succeed during your first year. These ideas include telling you how to seek assistance, the questions you should be asking, and the answers you should be receiving. Finally, in **Section 12** we share our ideas about what a master teacher believes and what he or she does with students that warrants the *master teacher* label.

Our Point of View

Before we begin, we also want to share our point of view with you. In planning the contents of this manual and in deciding the specific strategies and techniques to include, we could have compiled a collection of many different ideas drawn from a variety of sources, with no consistent underlying foundation to them—the "eclectic" approach, if you will. These ideas might be cute, innovative, and entertaining, but they might also be seriously lacking in one very important way: support in scientifically based research. There is nothing wrong with being eclectic when it has to do with food tastes, clothing styles, movies, music, and so

on. When it comes to teaching, however, we believe that being eclectic is very risky. An eclectic has been defined as "one who has his feet planted firmly in mid-air," and we are determined that this will not be the outcome for the users of *The Tough Kid New Teacher Kit*. We want you to have your feet planted firmly on the ground, confident in your knowledge of proven behavior management practices, and well on your way to becoming proficient in their use.

This manual's emphasis on creating a structured environment for your students is another big part of the firm foundation we hope to build. Most people agree that structure is important for children and adolescents. However, there is less agreement about what structure means. By structure, we are referring to a predictable and consistent learning environment where students know that there is a clear and unambiguous relationship between their behavior and the consequences of their behavior.

Don't be misled by the word "consequence." We are not referring to dark and dire punishments for misbehavior. On the contrary, when we talk about consequences, the vast majority of the time we are talking about positive consequences for appropriate student behavior. We do not believe that a "structured" classroom is necessarily a "strict" classroom or that a teacher in a structured classroom should be a harsh

effort and achievement are expected, recognized, and reinforced.

disciplinarian. Such criticisms imply that structure suppresses freedom and creativity or that it is excessively punitive or negative in tone. When the term "structure" is used in this manual, it refers to the creation of a structured learning environment that offers a safe and secure place where effort and achievement are expected, recognized, and reinforced. A structured classroom is a classroom where the need for testing the limits is substantially reduced and where student frustration and agitation about unclear expectations are greatly decreased.

Providing a structured learning environment is one of the most difficult tasks a new teacher can work to master. However, we think the basic concepts and specific strategies and interventions described in this manual will provide you with enough of the right kind of information to get you off on the right foot for the coming school year.

> " *Providing a structured learning environment is one of the most difficult tasks a new teacher can work to master.* "

Section 2

Seat Belts Fastened, Tray Tables Up:

Getting Ready for Takeoff

It's August 1. You are back from an all-too-short summer break. You look at the calendar and realize that in about three weeks you will be reporting to a new job. You are going to be a teacher!

Teaching may be something you have wanted to do from an early age. It may be something you became interested in relatively recently. Or it may be something you just sort of stumbled into. Regardless, in less than one month, you will be responsible for teaching a classroom of all kinds of students: eager and reluctant learners; well-behaved and compliant students; tough kids who are noncompliant and anything but well-behaved; students on grade level; and students way below or way above grade level.

Some of you may not have even finished your teacher preparation program yet! Because of teacher shortages, you may have been hired based on your agreement to complete such a program. A few of you may have even been hired as a midyear replacement.

No matter what your situation, you may suddenly realize that you do not have the faintest idea of what you will do on your first day of school.

Maybe your education professors didn't touch on the subject, or your cooperating teacher during student teaching may not have talked about the first days of school very much. Friends who are teachers, or who *were* teachers, may not have been much help. You may have heard them say things like:

"You need to experience it to believe it."

"Words cannot describe it."

"It was all a big blur."

"Momma told me there would be days like this."

"I thought I was ready for it."

Comments like this are not helpful, whether they are from your personal friends or the thirty-year veteran down the hall. They undermine your confidence, and they may reinforce the idea that taking effective action is not possible. In fact, many of the statements made by these teachers are myths! While such myths may be entertaining, there is usually no basis in fact for them.

Your lack of preparation for your first few days and weeks as a teacher may provoke more anxiety if you have been assigned to one of the more difficult schools in the school system. Don't feel like you are being singled out, however. New teachers *are* often given the toughest assignments in the toughest schools with the toughest kids to teach. And many of them do a phenomenal job!

You may have already received your invitation from the school system to attend a one-day orientation for new teachers. Typically, most of this time will be spent on school system policies and procedures, including information about insurance coverage, retirement contributions, and rules governing sick days and personal leave days. This is all very important, to be sure. But you are right to worry that this orientation day is not going to help you prepare for the first days and weeks you spend with your students.

Box 2-1

Meet Mrs. Muttner!

In this manual, we will give all the unhelpful teachers in the universe a name. Meet Mrs. Muttner, our mythical teacher. Mrs. Muttner can, metaphorically, be either a man or a woman. You are bound to meet Mrs. Muttner in your first teaching position, because she is in almost all schools. Mrs. Muttner is the self-appointed expert and resident critic in your school. She has an opinion on just about every aspect of the school, including the students, their families, the principal, the other staff, and, especially, new teachers. Mrs. Muttner can best be described as opinionated, negative, and critical of just about everything. She always has reasons why strategies will not work with your students and why you should not even try them!

Mrs. Muttner is loaded with what we call "Muttnerisms." Muttnerisms are judgmental statements that Mrs. Muttner is more than willing to share with you. Muttnerisms can be identified by their critical nature regarding how bad the students are, how much better the good old days were, how far below standard the school is, and, of course, how much she is undervalued. An example of a Muttnerism is, "Don't smile 'til Christmas. It'll show 'em who's boss."

Be careful. Mrs. Muttner may seem like she wants to help you in your new job, but she is a morale killer. Muttnerisms have been included throughout this manual. However, we will remind you regularly not to believe Mrs. Muttner! Instead of spending time with Mrs. Muttner, look for a true mentor teacher to help you. He or she is also easily recognized. True mentor teachers are organized, have great classroom management skills, and love teaching as a career. They are positive about their students, are optimistic about the school and staff, and are genuinely interested in helping you. Hang around these teachers, ask their advice, and invite their input. They will be an immense help to you. Caution though: Mrs. Muttner will not approve....

The Importance of the First Few Days

It may be exaggerating a bit to say that your first few days as a teacher will "make you or break you," but there are certainly elements of truth in this statement. Researchers who have carefully studied this time have found consistently that the first few days of school have a profound impact on both teachers and students alike (Evertson et al., 1997; Emmer et al., 1997; Moran et al., 2000). A well thought out, forward looking plan, executed competently, is associated with positive academic and behavioral outcomes for students. The reverse is also true. A chaotic and poorly planned first few days sends the wrong message to students about the importance of learning and hard work.

There are many questions you will need to ask yourself before the school year begins. They are basic questions you may have already thought about, but now it is getting close to zero hour, and you are running out of time to answer them:

- **What is the main message you want to send your students in the first few weeks?**

  You want them to view you as a confident, organized teacher whose main job is to teach them as much as you possibly can.

- **How do you want your classroom to be viewed by your students?**

  You want your students to think of your classroom in very positive terms. You want them to think of it as an enjoyable place where they can experience success and learn a lot. You want them to view your classroom as a place where they can be comfortable and work hard at the same time. You want them to see it as a place where they can achieve a great deal as a result of your careful planning and systematic and purposeful teaching.

- **What do you need to do so that your students will answer these questions the way you hope they will answer them?**

  There's an old military saying that claims, "All battles are won before they are fought." We don't mean to imply that the first few days of school are just like D-Day or Desert Storm. We do mean,

though, that you must be prepared to devote time, effort, and thought to making these first few days as smooth as possible.

The next few pages address a number of very important decisions that must be made *before* the first day of school. How to arrange the physical design of your classroom to create an environment conducive to learning will be the first topic. Issues to consider in setting up a schedule of activities will then be discussed. This section closes with a final "week before school" list of reminders to consider as you count down to the first day of school.

Kicking the Tires and Making Sure the Wings Are Attached

A classroom with a well-designed physical layout increases student learning and helps to promote higher levels of appropriate student behavior. How you plan the room layout will significantly affect your teaching and your students' learning and behavior. This task should definitely *not* be an afterthought on your preparation and planning list.

There are a number of decisions that need to be made about classroom design, all of them with only one goal in mind—to increase the likelihood that students will learn. These are the issues that you will need to address and consider:

- First things first! Do you have a classroom that is yours and yours alone? Or will you be sharing a classroom with one or more other teachers? If you will be sharing, arrange to meet with your new "roommates" as soon as you can to discuss the issues on this list.

- Place your desk in an area of the classroom where you won't be tempted to sit at it much. Very little effective teaching occurs when a teacher is sitting at his or her desk, and behavior problems have a better chance of escalating then as well. During school hours, you may even want to pretend that you do not have a desk at which to sit! **We are really not kidding about this**!

- Set up your classroom to allow space and routes for you to move about without squeezing by furniture or hurdling over objects in the

Don't sit at your desk while teaching

Figure 2-1

Not Too Much Desk Time

way (Moran et al., 2000). Good teachers **move around and circulate almost nonstop when they are monitoring student performance**. Easy movement about the classroom is also essential for *proximity control*, a basic and frequently used behavior management strategy where a teacher moves close to the students who are behaving inappropriately or who even look like they are about to behave inappropriately.

• Set up your classroom space with good sight lines that will allow you to observe all students from everywhere in the room. Good sight lines are essential for monitoring students' behavior and so your students can see you at all times.

• Adopt a policy of *moderation* for what you hang on your wall space (Jones, 2000). While you don't want to *underdo*, don't overdo either! Your time will be at a premium during this period, and we believe it is better spent on planning activities essential to learning, rather than on elaborate bulletin board displays that may only serve to distract some of your students. You will, however, need to plan adequate space on the walls for your classroom rules and What If? Chart (discussed in **Section 5**), student work, and your classroom schedule and assignments.

• Plan on assigning seats to your students on the first day of school. Put nametags on the desks before class starts so everyone will know where to sit. This is another way to show your students that you are prepared to take your teaching and their learning seriously. Change assigned seating as needed after school starts so that you can separate the noisy, disruptive, noncompliant troublemakers. Allowing them to sit together is like grouping students by disruptive behavior

ability. Arrange seating so that they can be separated from each other and kept close to you (Remember proximity control?).

Classroom Scheduling for Takeoff

How classroom time is organized and used is another important factor affecting student learning and behavior. Reliable findings in educational research clearly establish the link between *time available* to learn, *time spent* in learning activities, and the *actual learning that takes place.* Also, the more time students spend actively engaged in learning activities, the less time they have available to misbehave! To use time well, incorporate the following ideas as you create a classroom schedule:

> ❝ *The more time students spend actively engaged in learning activities, the less time they have available to misbehave!* ❞

- In your initial schedule, draft a list of activities that you anticipate using. Examples for an elementary classroom might include taking the roll and lunch count, reading/language arts time, math, and so on. Examples in a secondary class might include taking roll, homework collection, teacher lesson presentation, cooperative learning group time, and so on.

- Designate "start" times and "stop" times for each activity on your schedule. Allow for two to three minutes of transition time between each stop time and the next start time. Once you implement your schedule, be sure to start learning activities at the start time you have specified on the schedule. Do not start a new activity 13 minutes or even three minutes after the time you have designated. *Start when you say the activity will start.* If you start on time, you will send an important message about preparedness to your students. If you do not start on time, you will also send a message to your students—one you probably do not want to communicate. Remember, the behavior that you model is the behavior that you get.

Scheduling several shorter learning activities in a time period is often preferable to scheduling a single, longer learning activity,

[handwritten margin note: The more time students are actively engaged in learning the less time they have to misbehave.]

especially for younger students. However, be careful not to overschedule either. A minute-by-minute schedule will be too much for you and your students to handle.

- Avoid "down time" in the schedule and periods of time when no learning activity is planned. Down time is often a trigger for inappropriate behavior, and it wastes valuable learning time.

- Discourage unplanned interruptions as much as possible (Wong & Wong, 1998). In any school, on any given day, there can be a myriad of interruptions. Tell everyone you see, as politely and as sincerely as you can, that you are trying your best to maximize available learning time. Tell them that you prefer that nothing interrupt your teaching and your students' learning. You may even want to post a note outside your classroom door that says, unless it is an emergency, to please come back later when the students are not in class. Your note will indicate that you want to make the best use of time and unnecessary interruptions put a big kink in those plans. Having even a short conversation at the classroom door with someone can also allow misbehavior to get off the ground.

Other Procedures Related to Time

There are several other procedures related to time and scheduling that you can think through and use. These have more to do with organizing the schedule and how you have your students move through the schedule.

- Every day, before class starts, organize what the schedule requires in the way of lesson materials and supplies, manipulatives, teaching manuals, and so on. One of the biggest time-wasters in schools is the time teachers spend shuffling through papers, manuals, and piles on their desks to find their lesson plans for that day or hour. If you don't show your students that you are serious about being organized and

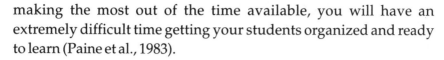

making the most out of the time available, you will have an extremely difficult time getting your students organized and ready to learn (Paine et al., 1983).

- Think through and develop a plan for distributing things like learning materials, graded assignments, and notes home to parents. During the first days of school, have your class take the time to actually practice these routines until they are performing them in a timely and efficient manner. Failure to develop and practice these procedures unnecessarily fritters away valuable time and provides a fertile environment for more behavior problems. Trust us when we say that the time spent in practice now will pay off huge dividends *later* with a routine that runs smoothly (Witt et al., 1999).

- Plan on actively teaching your students how you want them to move from one activity to another or from one area of the classroom or school to another (Paine et al., 1983). This means thinking through each move ahead of time. You might plan to say something like, "Class, when I say, 'Return to your seat,' I want you to leave the group one at a time and walk quietly back to your desk." Or you might say, "When I ask you to line up at the door, I want you to push your chair in and walk quietly, with no pushing and shoving. I want you to do that in 90 seconds." For each procedure in your entire schedule, you will give specific directions, demonstrate the procedures, and have your students practice following them. Encourage and give feedback, making certain to verbally recognize good performance.

To summarize, we can't emphasize enough the importance of your classroom schedule and attending to the procedures and routines that relate to it. Time is a precious resource. You can never get enough of it, and you cannot recover time that is wasted. When it comes to student learning, "Use your time wisely" is not a cliché.

Oh, for heaven's sake. You shouldn't spend all that time going over routines. The kids should already know what they're supposed to do!

Don't believe Mrs. Muttner!

Taxiing Down the Runway

The first day of school is now five days away, and, as if setting up a classroom, drawing up a schedule, and developing classroom rules and a management system (next section) were not enough, there is still much to be done in order to make the first day and the first few weeks go smoothly:

- Make contact with your new students and their parents ahead of time, where possible. Short, personalized notes or postcards, an open house at the school, or phone calls will buy a lot of good will. "Banking" good will before the school year even starts can pay off big time when you may really need it later in the school year.

- Decide what you will do and say the first minute and the first hour of the first day. What kind of introductory impression do you want to make? Plan an engaging and novel learning activity as your very first activity of the first day.

- Make sure that you have all of your classroom materials ready for use. These are things like paper, pens, pencils, and books. Decide where you are going to store things and who will have access to storage areas.

general place for paper and pencils for students use.

- Make sure that you have enough desks and chairs for all of your students. This may sound rather odd, but stranger things have happened on the first day of school. *Starting the school year on a big-eventually desks?*

- Seek the assistance of experienced teachers, area coordinators, or district office personnel to help you come up with a list of high-quality curriculum materials. Don't go on a spending spree with allotted classroom funds without first checking with colleagues who have had more experience in identifying sound curriculum materials. With the recent passage of the "No Child Left Behind Act of 2001," there will be a greater emphasis in schools on using curriculum

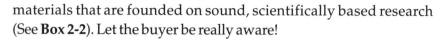

materials that are founded on sound, scientifically based research (See **Box 2-2**). Let the buyer be really aware!

Box 2-2

Scientifically Based Research

The term "scientifically based research" means research that involves the application of rigorous, systematic, and objective procedures to obtain valid and reliable information relevant to education activities and programs.

- Take a tour of your school. Most of your time so far has probably been spent either in your classroom or in a larger meeting room during faculty meetings. Become familiar with the physical layout of the entire school. Get comfortable with finding your way to and from common areas and your classroom.

  I done. I know my way around the school.

- Spend some time with your mentor (Hopefully, it is not Mrs. Muttner!). If you have already been assigned a mentor by your principal or school system central office and have not yet been contacted by him or her, initiate contact yourself. Ask if you can spend some time together before the start of school. When you meet, ask the questions you have been storing up. Share some of your worries and concerns. If you haven't been assigned an official mentor, seek out a veteran teacher in your school. Choose someone you can talk to comfortably and who will listen and offer reassuring advice and support.

  I have Ms. C.G. say no more. She's #1

- As the big day approaches, make sure you are getting enough rest to see you through the very busy and demanding days and weeks ahead. You will think better and make better decisions.

- Finally, here is one last suggestion for the first day of school. Plan on greeting your students at the door of your classroom with a smile and a positive comment. Ask them to find their desks (which you have already preassigned with nametags) and get ready to go to work and learn.

Box 2-3

Preflight Summary Checklist

- ❑ Contact your students and their parents ahead of time.
- ❑ Plan the first minute and the first hour of the first day in detail.
- ❑ Have all classroom materials ready for use.
- ❑ Have enough desks and chairs for all of your students.
- ❑ Order curriculum materials.
- ❑ Take a tour of your school.
- ❑ Spend time with your mentor.
- ❑ Get enough rest.
- ❑ Plan to greet your students at the classroom door with a smile and a positive comment!

These are just a few of the many items that will be on your "to do" list before school starts. We will deal with more in the pages ahead.

Section 3

Avoiding Turbulence:

Classroom Rules and Expectations

procedures
expectations

One of the most important decisions that will determine your success in the first few weeks on the job, as well as the balance of the school year, concerns your classroom expectations, or rules, for your students. Why are rules so important? Rules lay out your expectations for students. Make no mistake. Your expectations, stated in the form of rules, are the foundation on which your classroom will operate.

Good rules help prevent behavior problems, increase available, productive, learning time, and drastically reduce limit-testing by your students. Good rules, consistently enforced, provide students with a classroom structure that offers predictability and security and establishes a solid base for learning. Good rules offer a learning environment where effort and achievement are expected, recognized, and rewarded.

effort and achievement are expected, recognized, and rewarded.

Good Rules

What are the characteristics of good rules?

1. **There should be just a few rules and not a long list of "do's" and "don'ts."** Try to keep the number of classroom rules down to about five or six.

2. **The wording of the rules should be simple and straightforward.** An attorney should not be required to interpret the meaning and intent of your rules.

3. **The behaviors described in the rules should be observable and measurable.** This means that the rules should not be open to any number of interpretations due to vague language or lack of specificity. You should be able to count the number of times the behaviors described in the rules occur.

4. **The rules should be positively stated, where possible.** In other words, they should state what you want students *to do* ("start rules"), rather than what you *don't want them to do* ("stop rules"), unless this confuses the meaning of what you want. For example, "Don't spit" makes more sense than "Keep your spit in your mouth."

5. **The rules should focus on important student behaviors.** Important student behaviors are behaviors that are closely linked to student achievement and appropriate classroom behavior, that is, they are linked to *behaving like a student*. A "package of rules" that addresses important classroom behaviors, with examples, is described below:

A compliance rule—
- Follow the teacher's directions right away.
- Do what your teacher asks immediately.

> Always include a rule that clearly communicates your expectations about student reaction to your directions and requests. A rule that tells students that you expect them to follow your instructions immediately targets one of the biggest problems teachers, new and experienced, have with students: COMPLIANCE!

A preparation rule—
- Have books, pencils, and paper when you come to class.
- Have your homework completed when you come to class.

(handwritten margin notes:)

Rules:
compliance
- follow direction
  1st time asked
preporation
- have pencils
talking
- raise hand
- red/green light
behavior
- hands/feet to
  self
- In seat
transition
- move quickly
  and quietly

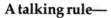

A talking rule—
- Raise your hand and ask for permission to speak.
- Talk to others only about the task at hand or during free time.

Box 3-1

The Red/Green Sign Program for Talking

Consider implementing the Red/Green Sign Program if you truly do not need hand raising in *every* instance in your classroom. (The Red/Green Sign you will need is provided in this kit.) Explain the program like this:

"Class, when the red side of this sign is posted (on a hook) at the front of the class, that means *no* talking unless you raise your hand and wait for my permission to talk. I will always tell you when the red sign is being posted. I will say something like, 'The red sign is up; remember to raise your hand to talk.' Usually the red sign will be up when I am teaching in front of the class, when we are having a class discussion, or when you are working individually on assignments at your desk.

"I will turn the red sign over and post the green sign when it is okay to talk quietly without getting my permission first. I will tell you when the green sign is going up. I might say something like, 'Green sign up; remember to talk quietly.' The green sign might go up when you are working on projects in small groups, when I am talking to someone who has come to the door, or when you have come back from lunch or recess and our next activity has not started yet."

A classroom behavior rule—
- Keep hands and feet to yourself.
- Leave your seat only with permission.

An "on time" rule—
- Be in your seat before the bell rings.
- Be in class by 8:00 a.m.

A transition behavior rule—
• Walk in the halls without talking or touching anyone.
• Put your work materials away in two minutes without talking.

As you formulate the rules for your classroom, feel free to use these rules as they are written or change them to meet your personal requirements. Avoid selecting rules like those in **Box 3-2**. These are rules that are vague and cannot be counted or measured. We often assume that students know what these rules mean, when, in reality, they do not.

Box 3-2

Examples of Poor Rules

• Respect authority.

• Take responsibility for your own actions.

• Demonstrate respect for others.

• Be a good citizen.

• Don't be noisy.

• Do your best.

• Maintain appropriate behavior.

6. **Rules should be posted in a conspicuous spot in your classroom on the laminated chart that is included in this kit.** The rules should be printed in letters that are large enough to be read from anywhere in the classroom.

Take Action to Teach Your Rules

rules
go over rules
every day
1st few
weeks-
review &
teach rules
often-

Developing or adopting a set of classroom rules that follow the guidelines we've just described is still not enough, however. Well-stated rules, written prominently on your rules chart, are just the first step. To be most effective, rules must be *taught* to your students. The key word here is *taught*. Not

Rules, schmules! I call 'em like I see 'em. These kids know what they're supposed to do without my having to spell it out!

Don't believe Mrs. Muttner!

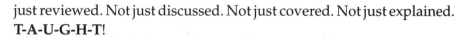

just reviewed. Not just discussed. Not just covered. Not just explained. **T-A-U-G-H-T**!

What is involved in teaching your classroom rules to your students? Teach rules to your students *actively* and *directly* in the same manner that you teach any other important concept or skill to your students:

- Describe and demonstrate specifically what you *mean* by each rule and what you *do not mean*. In other words, give lots of examples and nonexamples of what following or not following each rule looks like.

- Provide rule-following practice opportunities. Provide a lot of practice. Have the students role-play and rehearse the rules you have just explained and demonstrated. With younger students, pretend that you are a student and have students be the teacher and decide whether or not you are following the rules.

- Provide encouragement, corrective feedback, prompts, and reinforcement as needed.

- Practice some more and continue to provide feedback. Do this more than once. In fact, teach and reteach the rules over a number of days.

teach and reteach the rules over several days or the first few weeks.

Box 3-3

Rule Teaching Tip

Schedule a rule-following lesson each day during the first week of school, two or three times during the second week of school, and then pare down to only a "booster" session during the third and fourth weeks of school. Many teachers find it helpful to periodically teach such booster sessions throughout the school year.

We have prepared a sample script you may want to use to teach a set of rules to your students during the rule-following lessons. Notice that this script contains all of the important lesson elements present whenever any skill or concept is effectively taught—demonstration, practice, feedback, and more practice.

Box 3-4

Sample Script for Classroom Rule Teaching

What Teacher Says/Does	What Students Say/Do
"Today we're going to learn our classroom rules. First, we'll learn about one of the rules to follow when I'm teaching a lesson to you." (Point to the rule on the Rules Chart.)	
"The first rule is, 'Follow teacher's directions right away.'"	
"What is the first rule?"	"Follow teacher's directions right away."
"Right. That means, when I am teaching and I give you a direction, you should do it right away. This means you should start it within five seconds."	
"How soon is 'right away'?"	"Five seconds."
"That's right."	
(Proceed in the same manner through each of the rules on your Rules Chart. As you point to each rule, ask your students to read it out loud in unison.)	(If all the students do not respond in unison, require them to say the rule again until they do it correctly.)
"Okay. Now let's practice the rules. I'm going to go through each of the rules and give you a lot of examples of what following each rule might look like. Then I'm going to ask you to show me what following each rule looks like."	(After hearing description of each rule, students demonstrate what following the rule looks like.)
"Now I'm going to tell you what not following the rules is. I'm also going to show you what not following the rules looks like."	(Students demonstrate examples of not following the rules.)

Rules Summary

To review, good classroom rules are among the most important prerequisites to managing the behavior of your students and to maximizing learning. Remember these basic principles as you teach your rules to your students:

1. **Don't just tell your students what the rules are.** Show them what the rules mean by demonstrating what rule-following behavior *and* rule-breaking behavior look like.

2. **Don't fall for the mistaken notion that setting rules will make you seem like a tyrant or a "control freak" to your students.** Setting rules communicates your expectations about student behavior and achievement.

3. **Do not ever make a rule that you are not prepared to consistently enforce every time, every day.** Setting a rule and then enforcing it inconsistently or haphazardly communicates a great deal to your students. It tells them, in no uncertain terms, that there is no consistent relationship between what you say and what you do.

   You definitely do not want your students to receive this message!

Teaching Classroom Procedures

Your classroom rules are a statement of what you believe to be the critical student behaviors required to help students learn. They are as clear a statement as you can make about what you value in the classroom and what you expect from your students. It is more than likely, however, that your rules do not cover every important aspect of classroom life. There are a number of classroom procedures that you will need to teach your students to ensure that learning time is maximized (School Renaissance Institute, 2000) and that your classroom is a *positive* and *friendly* place to learn.

Some Important Classroom Routines and Procedures

- Gaining your attention.

- Requesting your assistance.

- Accepting negative feedback.

- Saying "please," "thank you," and "excuse me."

- Behaving appropriately during free time.

- Entering the classroom, and getting to work immediately.

- Keeping a neat and tidy work area.

One of the most neglected topics in schools today involves classroom routines and procedures (Witt et al; 1999). As educators, we tend to assume that students will know how we want them to get our attention without being told. Or we may believe they already know what the limits are for behavior during earned free time. Even after we have *told* our students these things, we may assume they have all the information they need to comply with our expectations. Wrong, wrong, wrong.

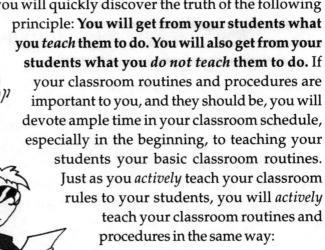

As a new teacher, you will quickly discover the truth of the following principle: **You will get from your students what you *teach* them to do. You will also get from your students what you *do not teach* them to do.** If your classroom routines and procedures are important to you, and they should be, you will devote ample time in your classroom schedule, especially in the beginning, to teaching your students your basic classroom routines. Just as you *actively* teach your classroom rules to your students, you will *actively* teach your classroom routines and procedures in the same way:

- Define and demonstrate what you *want* and *do not want*, using examples and nonexamples.

- Provide practice and rehearsal opportunities.

- Provide encouragement, corrective feedback, prompts, and reinforcement.

- Provide more review, then continued practice and feedback.

Devote the time and energy required to make sure your students know what the rules are and what the routine procedures are in your classroom. Investing time on this task now will pay big dividends to both you and your students in the long term.

Talk low, talk slow, and don't say too much.

Section 4

This Is Your Captain Speaking:

Talk Low, Talk Slow, and Don't Say Too Much

" Not following directions," or noncompliance from students, is one of the more aggravating problems that bothers teachers. So, in this section we are going to give you a technique that takes care of this problem. We will also show you how to improve the effectiveness of the disciplinary technique teachers in America use the most—the reprimand. Yes, it's true. According to the research conducted in this area, teachers from elementary grades through high school use reprimands far more frequently than any other disciplinary technique (Van Houten & Doleys, 1983). The trouble is, most of them do it wrong, and they do it far too often.

If you correctly use the technique we are about to give you, you will get about a 30 percent improvement in students' direction following. This is the case whether your directions are "to do" something or to "don't" do something. The secret is in how you make requests of your students. We call this method "Precision Requests." The technique reminds us of the old John Wayne adage: "Talk low, talk slow, and don't say too much."

Factors Affecting Compliance

Here are some of the factors that will make a huge difference in whether or not your students follow your directions:

1. **Do not use a question format when making a request.** Avoid wording your request like this: "Wouldn't you like to get started on that assignment now?" "Isn't it time you got to work?" or "Don't you think you ought to get that taken care of?" These are silly questions, because our real intention is not to give the student a true choice. Instead of a question, make a direct statement, something like, "Please start your assignment."

2. **Get close to the student when making a request.** The optimal distance is about three feet (or an arm's length). Do not make requests from across the room or from behind your desk. Requests made from a distance are much more likely to be ignored!

3. **Look the student in the eyes when you make a request** (Hamlet, Axelrod, & Kuerschner, 1984). You will almost always get eye contact back from the student when you are within a few feet of him or her. Whether or not the student gives you eye contact back, move closer until you are within the optimal three feet. Then make your request.

4. **Give the student enough time to respond.** A reasonable amount of time is five to 10 seconds. While this may seem like an eternity, *do not interact further with the student during this time!* The average adult will interrupt this five to 10 second period about 30 percent of the time, nagging the student by repeating the same request again or by giving "machine gun" requests—different, multiple, rapidly fired requests given without waiting for

> **You will almost always get eye contact back from the student when you are within a few feet of him or her.**

the student to respond to the previous one. Some students *need* the 5 to 10 second period, uninterrupted, in order to take in the request, to make sense of it, and to begin to respond (Forehand, 1977).

5. **Specifically describe what you want.** Effectiveness is increased by giving well-defined requests and not "global" ones. For example, you might say to the class, "Please clear everything off of your desks," instead of "Please get ready for lunch."

6. **Do not "nag" or make the request repeatedly.** Make the request twice. Then, follow through with a preplanned consequence. The more times you make a request, the *less* likely a student is to do it (Patterson, 1982)!

> When you see your kids doing what you asked, leave 'em alone. Let sleeping dogs lie!

7. **Remain calm and unemotional.** Yelling, threatening gestures, frustrated looks, contemptuous remarks, rough handling, or guilt-inducing statements serve only to reduce your effectiveness and cause you to lose the respect of your students. Remember that you are a profes-

Don't believe Mrs. Muttner!

sional. (Teachers who are not in charge of themselves should *not* be in charge of students who are not in charge of themselves!)

8. **Notice and verbally reinforce students when they follow through and do as you ask.** Social reinforcement costs nothing and is easy to give. If you do not recognize and reward compliance, it will decrease over the long term.

Precision Requests

A Precision Request incorporates all of the variables we have described above. It combines them together and adds a "signal word," usually the word, "*need*," if the request must be made a second time. **Figure 4-1** depicts the Precision Request sequence.

The steps involved in using Precision Requests are as follows:

1. Explain Precision Requests and their consequences to the students before actually beginning to use them.

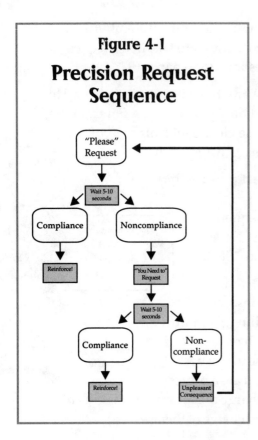

Figure 4-1

Precision Request Sequence

2. Make a quiet, direct "Please" request in a nonquestion format from within about three feet of the student.

3. After making the request, wait five to 10 seconds. Do not interact or nag (or make the request again) during this time. Just wait.

4. If the student does what you have asked (complies), socially reinforce him or her, even if you feel he or she should do it without being told. Say something like, "Hey, I appreciate it when you follow my directions," or "Good work for doing as I asked," or just give a simple, genuine "Thanks."

5. If the student does not comply with your first request, repeat it and add the signal word "need." "Need" is a signal word because it tells the student that this is his or her last chance. You are not going to make another request if he or she does not do as you have asked. Say something like, "Jackson, now I need you to stay in your seat."

(**Note:** It really does not make any difference if you say, "You need to...," or "I need you to...." What is important is that you consistently follow through after you make a "need" request.)

6. If the student *does* do as you have asked, verbally reinforce him or her. If he or she *does not* do as you have asked, follow through with a mild, unpleasant consequence from your What If? Chart (described in the next section).

7. After providing the unpleasant consequence, repeat the original request using the word "need." If the student does as asked, reinforce him or her. If not, follow through with the next unpleasant consequence listed on your What If? Chart.

To summarize, the use of Precision Requests ties back to the compliance rule on your classroom Rules Chart. The compliance, or "following directions" rule, is the most important rule on the chart. Precision Requests will greatly improve the odds that your students will do what you ask them to do as well as what you ask them to not do or to stop doing.

Section 5

Navigating the Trip:

The What If? Chart

ow that you have identified your rules and developed your plan
for teaching the rules to your students, you need to think about
what the consequences will be for following and not following
the rules. You can be assured that your students will be thinking about
the consequences. They will be wondering whether your rules will be
like so many other sets of rules they have listened to teachers talk about
throughout their school careers—empty words that do not carry much
meaning. In the past, nothing may have happened to them if they fol-
lowed the rules, and nothing may have happened if they did not. Most
of their teachers so far may have acted as if children *should* follow the
rules. They may have acted as if their students should behave appropriately just because they have been told what the rules are. Do not fall for
the "Should Myth" when you are trying to manage the behavior of your
students, especially your toughest students. You need to establish some
positive consequences for following the rules and some mildly unpleasant consequences for not following the rules. Most importantly, you
need to commit to consistently following through with both the positive

and the unpleasant consequences. If you do not follow through consistently, your rules will join the ranks of other empty words and rules your students have heard over the years.

There are a number of myths associated with consequences, and our archetypal teacher, Mrs. Muttner, is good at spreading them. We have already mentioned the "Should Myth": Students should behave because it is the right thing for them to do. In fact, tough kids frequently behave because of the *"could"* word. They think they "could" behave inappropriately and get away without a consequence.

> They should just behave. Let 'em know they have to behave or else!

Don't believe Mrs. Muttner!

The second myth of good teaching implies that the most effective consequences for students are unpleasant consequences. Not so, at least not in the long run. If you are setting up a systematic consequence system in your classroom, the best consequences for *permanent* behavior change for the better are *positive* consequences. The majority of consequences discussed in this chapter are positive. If your classroom consequences are mostly negative, your system will fail over time!

The third teaching myth is that *any* systematic consequence system is good as long as it uses both positive consequences for appropriate behavior and mild, undesired consequences for inappropriate behavior. Not so. Good consequence systems are *directly linked to the **rules*** in your classroom. Many teachers establish a set of classroom rules and then set up a consequence system that has nothing to do with the rules. If your rules are your minimum classroom expectations (as discussed in **Section 3** of this manual), then your consequence system should directly reward *following* the rules or provide mild, undesired consequences for *not* following the rules.

> What these kids understand is punishment! Let 'em know who's the boss from day one!

Don't believe Mrs. Muttner!

The What If? Chart

Your classroom rules are just empty words if you do not have consequences to back them up. As we have mentioned, this means *positive* consequences for following the rules and *unpleasant* or *undesired* consequences for not following the rules. It is this combination of consequences that will help your students learn to take seriously the expectations expressed in your classroom rules.

Hey, they get good grades when they do what they're supposed to do. And I just kick 'em out of class when they don't!

Don't believe Mrs. Muttner!

We suggest that you communicate the *positive* consequences of rule following and the *unpleasant* consequences of rule breaking with a What If? Chart. A laminated, wall-sized What If? Chart is provided in this kit. Your completed What If? Chart should be posted beside your classroom Rules Chart in a conspicuous place in the classroom. **Figure 5-1** shows an example of a completed What If? Chart.

Box 5-1

"Rule Following" as a Life Skill

In addition to creating an environment where you can teach and your students can learn, it is critical for your students to learn rule-following to be successful in life. There is virtually nowhere in our society where there are no rules or expectations. Your students will be expected to follow rules on the job, in a movie theater, while driving, in the community pool, on the beach, during a hospital stay, and at a friend's home. Think about it. Teaching your rules and expecting students to follow them helps to prepare them for life itself. Setting your rules aside or excusing students from following them does them no favors!

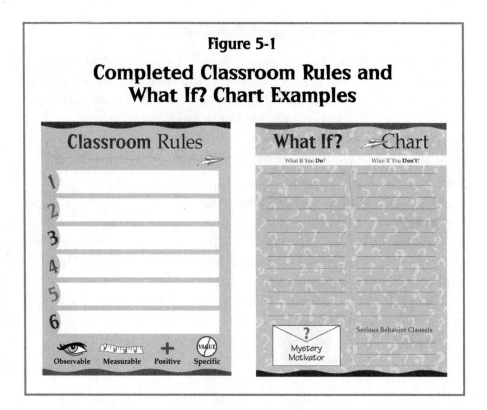

Figure 5-1

Completed Classroom Rules and What If? Chart Examples

Here is what you need to know to use your What If? Chart system:

1. The What If? Chart contains two columns. Facing the chart, the left side has spaces to list positive consequences for "What If You Do" follow the rules. The right column has spaces to list the unpleasant consequences for "What If You Don't" follow the rules.

2. The left side of the What If? Chart is the most important, because it includes rewards for following the classroom rules you have established. To help students buy in to the system, arrange a time at the very beginning of the school year when you invite them to raise their hands to suggest positive consequences they would like to earn. Tell students that the "Incentive Golden Rule" applies. Explain that this means that the reward items cannot take a lot of time or be too expensive. Using an erasable marker, list the activities and items they suggest and that you are also comfortable providing on the left side of the What If? Chart.

3. After you have invited class input for the positive consequences on the chart, explain Mystery Motivators. A Mystery Motivator is simply an incentive or reward that is written on a piece of paper and sealed inside a common, everyday envelope. Write a big question mark on the envelope with a marker, and tape the envelope to the bottom of your What If? Chart. (You can see a special place for a Mystery Motivator envelope on the chart.) Tell the class that there is something you have selected as a reward for following the classroom rules, but that you cannot tell them what it is. (It helps if you write something really special that you know the class likes on the paper in the envelope about every third or fourth use of the Mystery Motivator.) Check in *The Tough Kid Tool Box* on pages 3–6 for detailed instructions on how to set up Mystery Motivators and make them even more effective (Jenson, Rhode, & Reavis, 1994). **Box 5-2** has a list of potential rewards you can use in Mystery Motivator envelopes with elementary students. **Box 5-3** lists potential rewards for secondary students.

Positive Consequence Suggestions for Elementary Students

- Read a story to the class.
- Free time to talk (staying in seats).
- Play a group game.
- Earn a special activity.
- Snack for the class.
- View 15 minutes of a high-interest video.
- Drop a homework assignment.
- Lottery drawing for a prize.

- Reward Spinner (explained in **Section 6**).
- Chart Move (explained in **Section 6**).
- Send home a positive note with three randomly selected students.
- Small, inexpensive items from the Oriental Trading Company catalog (see below).

The Oriental Trading Company is a great resource for inexpensive, high-interest items (e.g., sticky, glow-in-the-dark eyeballs) that can occasionally be provided, or their use permitted, as a reward in the classroom. Request a catalog online at www.orientaltrading.com, call 1-800-875-8480, or write to the company at P.O. Box 2308, Omaha, NE, 68103-2308.

Positive Consequence Suggestions for Secondary Students

- Listen to the radio (class selects either the station or the volume, not both).
- Free time to talk (staying in seats).
- Snack for the class.
- Lottery drawing for a prize.
- Reward Spinner (explained in **Section 6**).

- Chart Move (explained in **Section 6**).
- Drop a homework assignment.
- Allow students to select seats for a day.
- Three positive postcards sent home with randomly selected students.
- Small, inexpensive items from the Oriental Trading Company catalog (see **Box 5-2**).

4. To determine whether the class earns a reward for following the classroom rules, you will also have to select a Secret Rules Number before the start of each school day. This is the total number of rules you will allow the class to break by the end of the day and still receive the reward. Each day before school starts, select the Secret Rules Number for that day. Tell the class that if they can keep the total number of rules violations below the unknown, or "secret," number, they will earn a reward. Tell them they can vote for one of the rewards you have listed on the left side of the What If? Chart, or they can choose to have what is listed in the Mystery Motivator envelope. (This adds real suspense to the system.)

Variation for Selecting the Daily Reward

Write each student's name on a slip of paper and place all the papers in a bag. When a class earns a reward from the left side of the What If? Chart, draw a name out of the bag. Allow that student to decide whether the class has earned one of the rewards listed on the chart or the Mystery Motivator posted at the bottom of the chart.

It is important that students do not know the Secret Rules Number. If they do know it, and the class breaks more rules than the number for that day, they will have no incentive to follow the classroom rules for the rest of the day. If the class goes over the Secret Rules Number, just say, "You can do better tomorrow," and have them go ahead with a planned academic task.

Some teachers have difficulty deciding on a Secret Number for the day. It is easy to pick one. Just look at your Rule Monitoring Chart (discussed later in this section) for the last week and figure out how many rules are broken on average each day. Then select Secret Rules Numbers that average one or two below that number. For example, if the average number of rules broken each day is 10, you might select the numbers 9, 12, 7, 11, and 6 for the week. These numbers average 9. As the class improves its rule-breaking behavior, gradually lower the Secret Rules Number until the class is not breaking more rules in a day than you can live with.

Technique Tip: If you are using this system with secondary students, you can use it across the whole week, rather than for the day. Then, on Friday, during the last part of class, reveal the Secret Rules Number to see if the class receives the reward. If the reward has not been earned (i.e. the number of rules broken for the week is greater than the Secret Rules Number), have the class work on the academic assignment you have planned.

Box 5-5

Secret Rules
Number Box Variation

Put about 30 slips of paper in a different bag with a number written on each slip. Each of these numbers represents a Secret Rules Number of the day. At the end of the day, randomly pick a slip and reveal it to the class. If the number of rules broken during the day is below the Secret Rules Number, the class receives a positive consequence. If the rules broken are higher then the Secret Rules Number, the class must work on an academic assignment, as usual, for the last 15 minutes of the day.

Box 5-6　Group Contingency Approach

The classroom management systems we have discussed so far reinforce the entire class for each student's behavior. This kind of approach is called a "group contingency." A group contingency is one of the most effective ways to manage classroom behavior. Instead of class members rewarding or reinforcing each other (on purpose or unintentionally) for misbehavior, a group contingency encourages students to reinforce each other for following the rules.

5. The consequences on the "What If You Don't" side of the chart are mild, unpleasant, or undesired consequences arranged in a hierarchy of increasingly more unpleasant consequences for breaking the rules. The unpleasant consequences you select for your chart should not require a lot of time and effort on your part to implement. However, they must be inconvenient or undesirable for the student. **Box 5-7** suggests some unpleasant consequences for the right side of your What If? Chart.

6. The first time each day a student breaks a rule, he or she earns the first undesired consequence in the hierarchy on the right side of the chart. The second time he or she breaks a rule, he or she earns the second one, and the third time, the third one.

7. Use what we call a Truth or Consequence Box for the fourth infraction on the What If? Chart. Place a piece of paper with one mild unpleasant consequence written on it in an envelope. Do this with about 20 different envelopes. Consequences can be repeated in several envelopes. Place the envelopes in a box (the Truth or Consequence Box). Stir and toss the envelopes so no one will be able to guess which consequence is in which envelope. When a student breaks four rules in one day, require the student to pick an envelope from the box immediately after the fourth occurrence. Whatever consequence is contained in the envelope is then implemented. The

Box 5-7

Examples of
Unpleasant Consequences

- Have the student remain at his or her desk for an additional 42 seconds (or some other arbitrary number) when the bell rings for class change, recess, lunch, etc., while everyone else is allowed to leave.

- Cut the first two minutes from the student's next recess.

- Have the student lose the right to take out equipment at the next recess.

- Require the student to eat lunch away from his or her friends.

- Call the student's parents to explain the problem behavior/rule infraction, and then have the student talk to his or her parents when you are through.

- Change the student's current seat assignment, and move him or her to a desk in front of your desk.

Box 5-8

Beware of Chronic
Rule Breakers

If a student breaks the classroom rules four times in one day and does it for three days in a row, you have a chronic rule breaker on your hands. Refer to **Section 8** for steps to take with chronic rule breakers.

Truth or Consequence Box is a simple strategy that (a) does not take up a lot of time and (b) adds an extra element of uncertainty to the "What If You Don't" side of the What If? Chart.

Technique Variation: When you explain this procedure to your class, ask students to suggest consequences for the envelopes. If you do this, take care that the consequences are not too severe or time consuming to carry out.

8. In addition to less serious classroom misbehaviors, extreme or dangerous misbehaviors can occur. A What If? Chart hierarchy must include a preplanned set of consequences for crisis or out-of-control behaviors. Crisis misbehaviors include blatant or intensely defiant noncompliance, a continuing physical fight, illegal drug possession, carrying a weapon, physical destruction of property (such as fire setting), or long duration tantrums that include yelling, swearing, or screaming. While these behaviors are rare, their crisis nature requires preplanned consequences that may temporarily remove the student from the classroom. **Box 5-9** includes examples of consequences you may list in the Serious Behavior Clause part of your What If? Chart.

Serious Behavior Clause
Examples for the What If? Chart

*   Student must go to another classroom for 20 minutes of Interclass Time Out (ITO) or in-school suspension.

*   Student will be escorted to the principal's office to sit for 20 minutes. The student must apologize and formulate a plan to improve his or her behavior in order to reenter class.

*   Student's parent will be called at home or at work to talk to the student on the phone about the behavior, or the parent will be asked to come to school.

*   Student will be suspended to home for one day for assault or substantial property damage. The police may be called.

9. Keep a Rule Monitoring Chart (located at the end of this section) on a nearby clipboard to keep track of which students have broken which rules each day. A reproducible monitoring chart is included at the end of this section for you to fill out with student names. Copy the completed chart, and start out with a fresh one each day. Each time a

student breaks a rule, place a tally mark alongside his or her name in the box that represents the rule number for the rule he or she has broken. Review the chart at the end of each day to identify chronic offenders in need of additional support.

10. There may be a "saboteur" who sets the whole class up for failure by chronic rule breaking. We provide suggestions in **Section 8** of this manual for how to deal with this problem. Do not worry! The techniques presented guarantee that the entire class will not be punished because of the misbehavior of a single student. In fact, a little later we will give you additional fun and potent ways to enhance rule-following behavior in the classroom.

Kids should just feel intrinsically rewarded and behave without bribes. You'll just make 'em dependent when you use artificial rewards.

Don't believe Mrs. Muttner!

If you are still wondering whether rewarding good behavior is a good idea, keep the following in mind:

1. We all work for something, whether it is a paycheck, the approval of others, or the satisfaction of doing a good job. It often takes an external reward or praise from others to "jump start" a student and to help him or her move toward a level of internal rewards.

2. Positive reinforcement and rewards are *not* bribes. Bribes are inducements for illegal or illicit behavior. Following classroom rules is not illegal or illicit.

3. Using rewards properly will *not* make a student dependent upon them. In fact, if rewards are used correctly in the classroom, they model incentive systems used in the real world, including those used in successful businesses.

Rule Monitoring Chart

Date _____

Student Names	Rule 1	Rule 2	Rule 3	Rule 4	Rule 5	Rule 6	Comments
1.							
2.							
3.							
4.							
5.							
6.							
7.							
8.							
9.							
10.							
11.							
12.							
13.							
14.							
15.							
16.							
17.							
18.							
19.							
20.							
21.							
22.							
23.							
24.							
25.							
26.							
27.							
28.							
29.							
30.							
31.							
32.							
33.							
34.							

Section 6

Traveling First Class:

Upping the Ante for Rule Following

A t this point, you may be wondering which technique you should use to help support and reward the rule following in your classroom. It is important to know that we do not expect you to use all of the techniques described in this section at once. In fact, far from it! To begin with, pick one that appeals to you and that you think your students will like. Set it up and plan to use it for several months or until the doldrums seem to be setting in. It is not unusual for this to happen in the month prior to or following the winter holidays. When this happens, and you want to spice things back up a bit, select a different strategy to try. Again, use it for a while until student interest needs a little tweak again, perhaps around spring break. Select another strategy, and begin anew. Of course, if student interest remains high, and the system you are using is working well, there is no need to change to a different strategy.

We would like to emphasize, though, that if you have been following the directions in this manual up to this point, you already have a basic

You will get more of the behavior that you recognize and reward in your students if you use positive reinforcements.

foundation laid for rule following in your classroom. The purpose of the techniques we will describe in this section is to increase the likelihood of rule following even further by "upping the ante." Positive consequences are the key to making this happen. How can this be? Think about the teachers or job supervisors *you* have had in the past. Which ones made you want to work harder or do a better job to please them? Most likely, these important people in your life set out clear expectations for your performance. They also provided you with helpful feedback, both of a corrective and positive nature. Remember how good that positive feedback felt? Remember how hard you were willing to work to get it? You probably wanted to do a good job, even when the person wasn't present or directly supervising you.

There is no doubt about it. Positive feedback and attention to a job well done leads to even more jobs done well. In other words, you will get more of the behavior that you recognize and reward in your students if you use positive reinforcement. If the majority of your attention is spent on correcting them, telling them what *not* to do, or what you want them to *stop doing*, these are

> **Positive feedback and attention to a job well done leads to even more jobs done well.**

the behaviors you will see more of in the long run. However, if the majority of your attention is in the form of praise and recognition for desirable behaviors and performance, these are the behaviors that will increase (Rhode, Jenson, & Reavis, 1992). **"Catch them being good"** are the key words of advice here. In this section, you will find a number of novel ways to accomplish this.

Reward Spinners

This system is wonderful to use with the Secret Rules Number system described in **Section 5**. A laminated game-type spinner is provided with this kit. Notice that the wedges of the spinner are of different sizes. With an erasable marker, write a reward you are willing to provide on each of the wedges. You will notice that one of the wedges is very "skinny." This is the wedge on which you should write something particularly desirable or big in comparison to the other wedges. Because this wedge is so small, the likelihood that students will stop on it is also quite small. Allow one of the students to take a spin (It must be a fast spin!) if the number of rules broken that day is below the Secret Rules Number. Whatever wedge the arrow lands on tells what the whole class receives as their reward for the day.

Box 5-5 Secret Rules # System

Technique Tip: Lay the spinner on a flat surface when the student spins the arrow so that it is truly a random spin. If you hold the spinner or have it on the wall, the arrow will tend to hit the lower wedges more often due to gravity.

Grab Bags

The Grab Bag approach is another simple reward system. To implement it, you will need a bag and about thirty pieces of paper (or 3" x 5" inch cards). On each paper or card, write the name of a reward. Make most of the rewards small, but write the names of three or four bigger rewards on the cards as well. If the number of rules broken is below the daily Secret Rules Number, mix up all the cards in the bag, and have the class pick one.

Technique Tip: Select a student to come up to the front of the class to draw a card. Have him or her close his or her eyes or look away while selecting the reward for the class. Picking a student for the Grab Bag choice enhances the motivating power of this technique. Also, be sure to periodically change the rewards written on the cards in the bag.

Chart Moves

This strategy is basically a "connect the dots" technique. (See **Figure 6-1**.)

To use Chart Moves, a student is picked to connect to the next dot each time the class keeps their rule breaking below the Secret Rules Number. When the class reaches a big dot, they earn a group reward. The reward can be preselected by the students or unknown to them. Or when they reach a big dot, you can provide a Mystery Motivator, a spinner, or a Grab Bag. To begin with, about every third day should be a reward day with a big dot. However, it is best to mix the big dots up so that there might be two small dots and then a large reward dot, then three small dots and a large dot, and then one small dot and a large reward dot. This variability helps to maintain motivation.

Chart Moves are especially useful when you want to reduce the rewards and not give them each day. Each connected dot represents one day. On average, at least every third day should be a big reward dot to begin with. However, over time you can gradually shift to have every fourth day, on the average, be a large dot reward day, then every fifth day and so on. It is still best to vary the number of small dots between large dots, however, to keep motivation high.

Chart Moves can also be used to offer rewards more frequently for following the classroom rules. Instead of having the Secret Rules Number revealed at the end of the day, you can use the technique several times during the day. For example, if the class breaks fewer than two rules each hour, they may be allowed to connect a dot. When they hit a big dot, they receive a reward. Remember, if you teach six hours a day and want to actually provide a reward only once on average per day for this technique, then you should use five small (non-reward) dots and then a

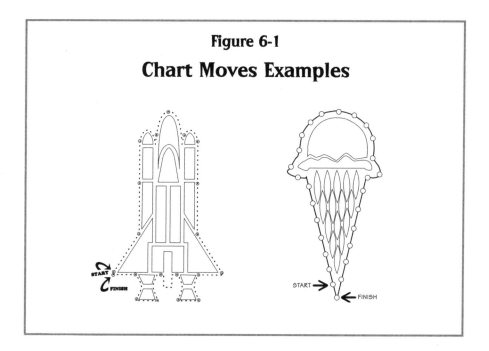

Figure 6-1

Chart Moves Examples

large reward dot. Similarly, if you want to give an average of two rewards per day, you will use two small (nonreward) dots for every large reward dot. (You will find reproducible Chart Move forms in The Tough Kid Tool Box, on pages 149–159 (Jenson, Rhode, & Reavis, 1994)).

Technique Tip: Make your Chart Moves picture large, and post it in front of the class. If it is big enough for students to see from their seats, each connected dot provides students with feedback about how well they are doing.

Remember: Students will only be motivated to behave if they are certain that their behavior will result in positive consequences!

Section 7

Going Supersonic:

Beyond the Basics

Do *not* use the techniques suggested in this section until you have your classroom rules and What If? Chart components (discussed in **Sections 3** and **5**) in place. This is a "baby steps" approach: small basic steps first and then the "beyond the basics" steps. We recommend that you pick only one of these "beyond the basics" programs to use at a time. It would be impossible to do them all at once. Pick one you like and start with that. One way to proceed that is popular with new teachers is to begin with the "Yes/No Program." This choice is very positive and effective, either alone or used in combination with a random signaling device (discussed later in this section).

Yes/No Program

This is a complete classroom management plan that ties right in with the classroom rules and the What If? Chart you have established. It is very easy to use. Here are the steps:

1. Make up about 30 "Yes" cards and about 30 "No" cards. (These can be copied from *The Tough Kid Tool Box*, pages 172–173.) It is helpful to copy the "Yes" cards onto a different color of paper than the "No" cards. For example, your "Yes" cards may be yellow and your "No" cards green.

2. Locate a clear container, such as a big jar or pitcher that students can see through.

> You don't need all those fancy things in your classroom. If you're a good teacher, they'll just behave!

Don't believe Mrs. Muttner!

3. **Now for the fun part!** At least three or four times per hour, catch a student following the classroom rules you have established. Each time you catch a student following a rule, put a "Yes" card in the container. You might say, "You raised your hand to ask a question! Thank you," or "Great following my direction immediately," or "You were in your seat before the bell rang!" Then follow up with, "You just earned a 'Yes' card for the class!"

    With colored cards, your students can see them building up in the jar. A big pile of yellow indicates that there are a lot of "Yes" cards in the jar. A big pile of green means a lot of "No" cards. Don't be surprised if you hear student comments like, "Come on, you guys; we have to earn more yellows!"

4. If a student breaks one of the classroom rules, identify the rule that has been broken. For example, you might say, "I'm sorry you are out of your seat. I have to put a 'No' card in the jar."

5. At the end of the day, select a student to come to the front of the classroom, look away, and pick a card. If a "Yes" card is selected, take down the Mystery Motivator envelope from the front of the class, making a big production out of it. Open the envelope, and allow the students to spend the last 15 minutes of the day or class period with the reward they have earned.

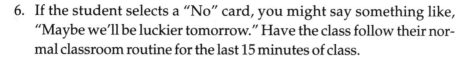

6. If the student selects a "No" card, you might say something like, "Maybe we'll be luckier tomorrow." Have the class follow their normal classroom routine for the last 15 minutes of class.

   Possible variation: If the student picks a "No" card, empty out the cards in the jar, and have the class count the number of "Yes" and the number of "No" cards with you. If there are more "Yes" cards than "No" cards, allow them to still have the Mystery Motivator.

7. If you are teaching junior high or high school students and have them for only one class period every day (or even every other day), run the program for an entire week and have the drawing on the last class day of the week. If they earn the Mystery Motivator, allow the students to have their reward during the last 15 minutes of that day.

8. If you are in an elementary setting, empty the container every day after the drawing. Do not carry cards over to the next day. Allow every day to be a fresh start. After you have emptied the container, have one or two students sort your "Yes" and "No" cards back into two piles for you. The only thing you have to do then to be ready for the next day is to put up a new Mystery Motivator envelope with the reward written inside of it. You will be all set to catch your students being good again. Rules on rule chart only!

   Technique Tip #1: Use the "Yes" and "No" cards to reward only the behaviors you have listed on your Rules Chart. Never use them for correct academic responses, because all of the students in the class may not be capable of doing well on a test or answering a certain question when called on. Also, do not use "No" cards for students who are incapable of following the rules. For example, if you have a rule that states, "Raise your hand to speak and wait to be called on," it would be unfair to award a "No" card to a student with Tourette's Syndrome (a neurological condition involving uncontrollable motor and verbal tics). This student would be incapable of withholding involuntary verbal bursts. If you have students who have not mastered the behavior or are just learning a new skill, pressure from peers may be too unfair and stressful. Also, if you have a saboteur in your class who breaks lots of rules, refer to the Chronic Rule Breakers section of this manual, **Section 8**, for advice on how to handle the situation. Saboteurs do not get to participate in the "Yes/No Program" until they have stopped setting their classmates up for failure.

Technique Tip #2: This tip has to do with the Preparation Rule on your Rules Chart. (This is your rule about what students are

expected to have with them to be ready to work. It refers to such things as having a pencil, notebook, textbook, homework, and the like.) Pick four students at random first thing in the morning when you are getting started. Have the students show you the things they need to have according to your Preparation Rule. If all four students are prepared, a "Yes" card goes in the jar. If any of them are not prepared, a "No" goes

in. You do not have to do this every day, but doing it two or three times a week (especially on Mondays) is effective at helping students stay prepared, since they never know the day on which you are going to do a spot check.

Technique Tip #3: Try using a random signaling device in your classroom. What does this mean? It means using something as simple as a kitchen timer that you can set to go off three or four times each hour. Set the timer for a different amount of time each segment, so that students won't know when it will go off. For example, set it for 10 minutes one time, 20 another, 5 another, and so on. Place the timer in a location where the students cannot see its face. When it goes off, scan the class and say something like, "Hey, you are all on task and following the rules. That just earned you a 'Yes' card."

Instead of a kitchen timer, you can make an audiotape with random beeps or bell rings on it and play it on a cassette player. Better yet, use the "Get 'em On Task" (GOT) program, described next.

Get 'em On Task (GOT) Program

If you have a computer in your classroom, this is an inexpensive software program you can use to help students get on task and stay on task.

Basically, what the program does is make the random sounds for you that cue you to scan the class and award a "Yes" or "No" card. You can set the program to have anywhere from 1 to 100 random sounds per hour. (We suggest three or four to start with.) Also, the GOT program can signal a random bonus sound that is different from the regular cuing sound. When the bonus sound goes off, scan the class as usual to see if all students are on task and following the classroom rules. If they are, award them *two* "Yes" cards in the jar. If they are not, still put just *one* "No" card in. In the beginning, we suggest one or two bonus sounds per hour to go along with your three or four regular cue sounds. Information on purchasing GOT software can be found in **Box 11-2** in **Section 11**.

Classroom Bingo

Also known as the Compliance Matrix, this program is very effective at improving compliance with classroom rules (Jesse, 1990). Typically, each bingo game is played across two or three days. To start with, we suggest using the 25-cell, laminated Classroom Bingo Chart provided with this kit. This chart has 25 squares, numbered through 25. Post the chart at the front of your classroom. Select a container (e.g., a paper bag or plastic jar), and place the small, laminated squares, numbered 1 through 25 (also provided in this kit), in the container.

When you notice one of your students following the classroom rules, draw a numbered square out of the container (or hold the container for the student to draw one). Using an erasable marker, make an "X" over the number on the bingo chart that corresponds to the numbered square that has been drawn from the container. For example, if the square with the number 18 on it has been selected from the container, you will mark an "X" on the box with the number 18 in it on your Classroom Bingo Chart.

When you use Classroom Bingo, students typically get quite excited as the rows and columns start to fill up and there are only a few empty boxes left. When a row or column is completely filled with "X"s, the class earns a Mystery Motivator. Once that happens, erase the bingo chart to begin again.

Technique Tip #1: You can combine the Classroom Bingo program with Get 'em On Task (GOT) or a random signaling device, such as a kitchen timer, for very powerful results! When the signal sounds, scan the class. If all the students are on task and following the rules, pick a number from the container and mark it on the bingo chart. If it is a bonus sound, pick and mark *two* numbers on the chart.

Technique Tip #2: When students are consistently successful with the 25-cell bingo chart, substitute the 49-cell Classroom Bingo Chart in its place. Add the additional cardboard squares with the numbers 26 through 49 (also provided with this kit) to your container. This is a good way to begin to reduce reinforcement. As you reduce reinforcement, students will need to produce more on "task and rule" following behavior to complete rows or columns and, thus, obtain their rewards.

Response Cost Lottery

This strategy is very effective for both elementary and secondary students (Witt & Elliot, 1982; Proctor & Morgan, 1991). To use it, divide your class into groups (e.g., all the students at a particular table or in a row). Give each group a name or number or allow each group to select their own name (the Eagles, the Dolphins, etc.). Provide an envelope for each team with the team name or number written on it. Post the envelopes where the students can easily see them and where you can conveniently access them. Place approximately five colored tickets in each envelope at the start of the day or class period. When a student breaks one of the classroom rules, say something like, "Angie, you're out of your seat. Your team loses a ticket." Then remove a ticket from the envelope posted for Angie's team.

At the end of the day, any team with at least one ticket left in its envelope is eligible to participate in the awarding of the Mystery Motivator. If all the tickets are gone, they do not.

In using Response Cost Lottery, it is critical to maintain a minimum of at least four praise or positive interactions with students for every negative interaction that results in removing a ticket from the envelope. This 4:1 ratio is needed to maintain a positive emphasis on appropriate behavior, rather than a negative focus on inappropriate behavior.

Technique Tip: After awarding the Mystery Motivator, have team members write their team name on any tickets they have left in their envelope. Gather up these remaining tickets and place them in a special container. Once or twice during the week, have a surprise "Blue Light Special." Mix up all the tickets in the jar, and pick one. Provide the team whose ticket you have picked with a special Mystery Motivator or other reward.

The "Sure I Will" Program

This social skills strategy is used in combination with Precision Requests (discussed in **Section 4**). It is very effective for further improving students' direction-following in your classroom (Martin-LeMaster, 1990). **Figure 7-1** depicts how "Sure I Will" fits into the Precision Request sequence.

To use "Sure I Will," first divide your class into groups or teams. Assign each team a positive response, such as "Sure I Will," "Okee-Dokee," "Glad You Asked," "Sure, Any Time," or "No Problem." Post each group's name on the blackboard.

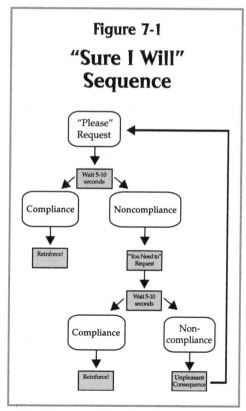

Figure 7-1

"Sure I Will" Sequence

Explain to the class that if you ask someone in their group to do something using a Precision Request, that student must respond with his or her group's assigned response (e.g., "Sure I Will") *and* do what you have asked him or her to. The student must give the response and do the request *before* you must repeat it using the cue word, "need." Each time a student successfully responds and carries out the request in this manner, you will place a mark on the board by his or her team's name. **Figure 7-2** depicts a blackboard example of "Sure I Will" Program teams.

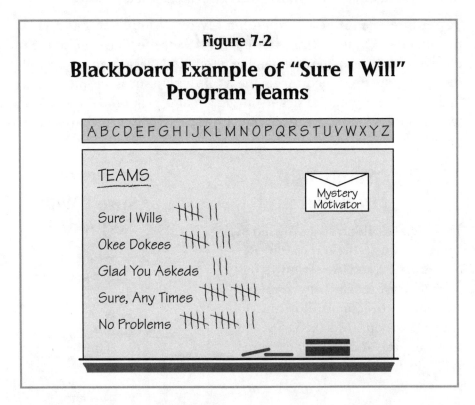

Figure 7-2

Blackboard Example of "Sure I Will" Program Teams

A B C D E F G H I J K L M N O P Q R S T U V W X Y Z

TEAMS

Mystery Motivator

Sure I Wills ||||| ||
Okee Dokees ||||| |||
Glad You Askeds |||
Sure, Any Times ||||| |||||
No Problems ||||| ||||| ||

Write a random number on the back of a Mystery Motivator envelope, and tape it on the board at the front of the class. At the end of the day, reveal the number to the class. Teams that have earned the same or a greater number of marks as the secret number get to participate in the Mystery Motivator. Teams that haven't earned the marks continue working. As with other strategies we have discussed, be prepared for

the occasional saboteur who sets up the group to do poorly. (This will be discussed in **Section 8**.)

Technique Tip #1: After this strategy is consistently working well, begin to reduce the reinforcement. That is, after a while do not put a mark up for every single "Sure I Will" or assigned positive team response. Tell the students you are only going to award marks for really good, sincere responses and that they won't know ahead of time when this will happen.

Technique Tip #2: This strategy is a very effective way to teach special education resource and self-contained classroom students a useful "teacher pleaser skill" that will help them be successful in their general education classrooms. You are teaching them to say "Sure I Will" and comply with requests when asked to do something.

Technique Tip #3: Some special education teachers have their students mark down on a card (or self-monitor) every time they remember to respond with "Sure I Will," "Okee-Dokee," or "No Problem" and do as asked during the time they are in their general education classroom. This helps the students remember to do as they are asked and to respond in an appropriate manner.

Section 8

Houston, We've Got a Problem:

Chronic Rule Breakers

Okay, your rules have been selected, taught, and posted. Your What If? Chart has been designed, hung, and implemented. You have "upped the ante" with additional positive reward systems. Still, some of your students may consistently break the classroom rules. Neither the positive nor the unpleasant consequences posted on the What If? Chart seem to capture their attention or interest and do not seem to improve their compliance on a consistent basis. What next? Something more is definitely needed for these students. To begin with, we suggest a Rules Self-Monitoring program (see the Self-Monitoring Classroom Rules chart at the end of this section).

If additional strategies are still needed after you have the Rules Self-Monitoring program established, we suggest that you try one or more of the additional strategies described in this section.

Rules Self-Monitoring

Here is how this program works:

1. Tell the students that when they break three or more rules in a day, they will be ineligible to participate in the class What If? Chart. Instead, they will be placed on a self-monitoring program.

2. Tape a copy of the self-monitoring chart to the chronic rule breaker's desk.

    Some kids are just bad kids. Don't waste your time!

    Don't believe Mrs. Muttner!

3. In each square of the chart, list the rules that the student is consistently breaking.

4. Teach the student how to monitor and evaluate his or her behavior each day by rating his or her rule-following behavior on a 1 to 4 scale (1=Needs Improvement, 2=Barely OK, 3=Average, 4=Great) on a regular basis. This may be at the end of a class period for secondary students or two times each day for elementary students, usually at the end of the morning and at the end of the afternoon.

5. Give the student feedback about the accuracy of his or her rating by putting one slash mark across the circled rating if you agree with it. Put an "X" across the rating if you disagree with it. Each time the student rates his or her behavior, you will *also* need to rate his behavior and give feedback.

6. Do not argue with the student about ratings. If he or she tries to argue about them, give him or her a Precision Request, such as, "I need you to *not* argue with me about this."

7. When the student has given him or herself four ratings with a "3" or above, and you have agreed with him, take the student off the self-monitoring program and place him or her back on the What If? Chart system with the rest of the class.

Box 8-1 Self-Monitoring Program Tip

A copy of the student's self-monitoring chart listing the rules on which he or she is working can be sent home to parents as a Home Note to be signed and returned the next day.

Interclass Time Out

Introduction. For very difficult students, additional strategies may need to be used in addition to a Rules Self-Management program. Interclass Time Out (ITO) is a very powerful option and can be a very effective intervention with tough classroom behaviors, such as back talk, calling the teacher a name, arguing, blatant defiance, fighting, and purposely damaging or destroying property. In many cases, ITO can all but replace out-of-school suspensions. This is desirable so that students can remain where they should be—in school, learning!

Foundation. There are several basic concepts to keep in mind when using ITO effectively:

1. The "time out" part of ITO is actually "time out from positive reinforcement." To work, ITO must be set up so that it is not a reinforcing, fun, or enjoyable place to be.

   > I have one rule: It's my way or the highway.

2. Place students in ITO as soon as possible after the inappropriate behavior that earned it. Immediate placement after the behavior that earned it will make its use more effective.

3. Assign the least amount of ITO likely to be effective in deterring the student from engaging in the problem behavior again. In other

   Don't believe Mrs. Muttner!

   words, don't use an elephant gun when a peashooter will do! Not only does less time make supervision easier, but it also keeps the students in the classroom as productive learners.

4. As a condition of their release from ITO, students should be required to work on and complete classroom assignments they are missing during ITO. If students are expected to do nothing for prolonged periods of assigned ITO, further misbehavior may be encouraged.

Additionally, when their assignments are all completed, students will return to class with a greater chance of success and will be prepared to participate in what is being taught. Parents are also likely to be supportive of ITO when the work completion of their (sometimes poor) student is monitored.

Getting Started. There are two main options for ITO procedures to be carried out as an intervention for your students.

Option 1: The principal implements the ITO for you. When the principal (or counselor or other available school staff member) is willing to implement ITO for teachers, it is the desirable choice. In this case, participating teachers are asked to place a student desk and chair in an isolated part of their classrooms. When ITO is earned, the teacher notifies the principal (usually by a note sent to the office with another student or by a brief message over the intercom). The principal then escorts the tough kid to another classroom for his or her assigned ITO.

a. The teacher prepares the student's needed materials (books, worksheets, paper, and pencil) for work he or she will miss. The principal returns to pick up the materials and deliver them to the student in ITO.

b. The principal monitors the student's behavior while in ITO, checks for assignment completion, and determines when the student is to be released from ITO.

c. When ITO time has been completed, and the student is released to return to his or her own classroom, he or she should be integrated back into the ongoing activities in a low-key, positive, and

unobtrusive manner. This means no lecture or drawing attention to the fact that he has served ITO time. A simple statement, such as, "Rocky, we're on page 23 in math. Please take your book out," is appropriate. As soon as possible, without interrupting your flow of instruction, stop by Rocky's desk to help him orient to the task as hand. Encourage him and praise him for his efforts to get back to work.

Option 2: You and at least one other teacher have an agreement to "house" each other's students for ITO. (Tip: Don't make an ITO agreement with Mrs. Muttner. It won't work!) If you have a principal who is unwilling to become involved in ITO but is still willing to support your use of it, solicit one or more other teachers with good classroom management skills to work with you to implement ITO. Again, you will each need to supply a student desk and chair in an isolated area of your classroom away from other students.

a. Arrange a way to communicate with one of your ITO partners when a student has earned ITO. This may be as simple as a note carried to that teacher by another student, telling her to expect the student within three minutes. If you have an intercom system, you can call the office and ask the secretary to notify the teacher that a student is on his or her way to the designated ITO classroom.

b. When the ITO classroom is within sight of yours, you and the receiving teacher can both step to your doorways and observe the student making the transition. When the classrooms are further apart, a prearranged escort may be needed. Possible escorts are a school counselor, an office worker, an aide, or other appropriate school personnel.

c. The "sending" teacher collects materials needed for assignment completion as soon as possible and has a student carry them to the "receiving" ITO teacher for the tough kid.

d. The receiving teacher will need to monitor the student and make sure that he or she follows the ITO rules. The teacher will also excuse the student when his or her time is up. Again, if the student needs an escort, prearrange how this will take place.

e. When the student has completed his or her ITO time and the receiving teacher sends him or her back to his or her own classroom, the student should be reintegrated into class unobtrusively, in the same manner described above.

Technique Tip: The effectiveness of ITO is greatly enhanced when the student who has earned ITO is sent to a *different* grade level to complete it. When feasible, a receiving ITO room that is two or more grade levels different than the student's assigned grade is best. In this case, the student is less likely to have good buddies in the receiving classroom and is less likely to continue acting out with an audience of students who are significantly older or younger.

Plan Ahead of Time. There are several things you will need to take care of before you begin to use ITO.

1. **Inform students ahead of time of the behavior expectations while they are in ITO.** Make certain students understand them. Typical rules for ITO are simple:

    a. No noise or talking to other students.

    b. No sleeping.

    c. Stay in your seat.

    d. Work on your schoolwork.

Post the rules beside the student desk provided for ITO recipients in an easy-to-see spot.

2. **Inform students ahead of time what will occur if they break ITO rules.** Generally, it is appropriate to add 10–15 minutes of time for each ITO rule violation, depending on the age of the student and the severity of the problem. If a student continues to break ITO rules (after three times), it is appropriate to invoke the Severe Behavior Clause on your What If? Chart. Typically, this will mean removing him or her from the ITO room and involving the principal. (**Note:** Under these circumstances, it is customary for earned ITO to be doubled, for parents to be notified, and for the student to serve out his or her time in isolation under the principal's supervision.)

3. **Preplan what you will do if a student earns ITO and refuses to leave the classroom when asked to do so.** Usually students will go to the receiving ITO classroom when they are asked to do so. However, there may be an occasional situation when a student refuses to go. Make arrangements ahead of time for another adult to come to your classroom immediately, upon notification, should this occur. The adult can be a counselor, school psychologist, principal, or vice-principal who has been trained in this role. The adult should enter the classroom, stand next to the student, and quietly and calmly ask him to leave. If he still does not, the adult should take a seat right next to the student. No further conversation should take place. Periodically, the adult should again ask the student to leave the classroom for ITO. Until the student actually does leave, the extra adult serves as a beefed-up form of proximity control.

Cautions in Using ITO. Use of ITO, as with all components of classroom and school behavior management systems, must follow due process procedures.

1. Students must know ahead of time what the rules are and what will happen if they break them.

2. Be certain to follow school and district guidelines/policies.

3. Inform parents about your classroom management system (including ITO) ahead of time. This can be accomplished on Back-to-School Night or by including written information to parents with registration materials. Encourage them to ask questions and voice concerns *before* problems arise.

4. Take care not to confuse assigning reductive consequences to students with denying them their basic rights. For example, it is not appropriate to deny a student access to the restroom, the telephone, or lunch.

5. Keep accurate data on the use of ITO with your students. At least once a week, evaluate the data for individual students and for the class as a whole. Is it working? Are more ITOs earned during certain activities or at certain times of the day, at least by one or more students? If ITO is working, you should not see an increase in the number of classroom rules being broken on a regular basis. If you are seeing more rules broken, this is a cue for you to figure out why. If students are regularly earning ITO at certain times of the day or prior to or during certain activities, they may be telling you they prefer ITO to remaining in the classroom during those times. Make adjustments in your classroom to correct these problems; for example, you can switch a subject from before lunch to after lunch.

Home Notes

The Home Note Program is another one of the most effective techniques for improving students' motivation and classroom behavior. This strategy involves regular communication between your classroom and the student's home. The Home Note Program consists simply of a note that (1) is periodically completed by the teacher; (2) is an assessment of academic and/or behavioral progress; (3) is sent home for the parent(s) to review, apply appropriate consequences to, and sign; and (4) is then returned to school. **Figure 8-1** shows a completed Home Note example.

The steps in setting up and implementing a Home Note Program are listed below:

Step 1: Design or select a simple home note. (Reproducible samples are included in *The Tough Kid Tool Box*, pages 41–47.)

Step 2: Decide which behavior(s) will be targeted for change. Limit the selection to no more than five academic and/or social behaviors.

Step 3: Make contact with the student's parent(s) either in person or by phone to gain their cooperation and to explain the system. With parental input, determine what positive or mild reductive consequences the parents are willing to deliver at home depending on the student's Home Note performance. Ask the parent(s) to read the note each day, make certain it is initialed by the teacher, and sign it to indicate that they have read the note. Convince the parents to accept no excuses from the student who doesn't bring the note home.

Step 4: Decide when the Home Note Program will start and how frequently Home Notes will be given. It is generally more effective to begin by giving the Home Note each day and then gradually decrease to giving the note only on Fridays (and, finally, to no note).

Step 5: Explain the program to the student, and answer any questions the student has about the program.

Step 6: Implement the program. After marking the note, give the student specific feedback as to what he or she did right and what needs improvement. Encourage the student!

Figure 8-1

Completed Home Note Example

My Weekly Home Note							

Name: Rocky Jenson   Week of: 3/19

Subject(s) or Behavior(s)		MON	TUE	WED	THUR	FRI	Comments
Begins Assignments Promptly		G	A	A			
Works Quietly on Assignments		G	G	A			
Follow Classroom Rules		A	G	G			Really has learned to follow rules
Is Prepared With Proper Materials		U	A	A			Forgot his notebook on Monday
Arithmetic		A	U	G			Did not pay attention on Tuesday—Talked
Reading		A	A	G			
Spelling		G	A	G			

Rating Scale	G = Great	A = Average	U = Unsatisfactory

Parent's Initials	MON	TUE	WED	THUR	FRI
	BJ	BJ	BJ		

Any homework?   Math problems, even, page 163

Any upcoming tests?   Spelling test on Friday

Any missing work?   Needs to hand in Indian project

Step 7: Once the program has been implemented, call the parent(s) at least twice the first week and once a week for the next two weeks to troubleshoot problems and provide support to the parent(s) for their part in the program.

Step 8: After the program has been in place for four to six weeks, arrange for another parent conference or talk with the parent(s) by phone to review the student's progress. Be optimistic and emphasize the gains the student has made. Discuss any concerns you or the parent(s) have with the program, make any needed adjustments, and plan to continue the program as needed.

Hey, the parents are even worse than the kids. They'll never follow through!

Don't believe Mrs. Muttner!

Troubleshooting Home Notes

As is the case with any intervention, problems can come up with the use of Home Notes. Common problems and their solutions, as well as tips for making Home Notes even better, are discussed in more detail in *The Tough Kid Tool Box*, pages 29–34.

Self-Monitoring Classroom Rules

Classroom Rules	Morning	Afternoon
_____	1 2 3 4	1 2 3 4
_____	1 2 3 4	1 2 3 4
_____	1 2 3 4	1 2 3 4
_____	1 2 3 4	1 2 3 4
_____	1 2 3 4	1 2 3 4
_____	1 2 3 4	1 2 3 4
_____	1 2 3 4	1 2 3 4
_____	1 2 3 4	1 2 3 4

Rating Scale (circle a number): **1** = Needs Improvement, **2** = Barely OK, **3** = Average, **4** = Great

If the teacher **agrees** with the student rating, put a line across the circled rating (⊘).

If the teacher **does not agree** with the student rating, put an X across the circled rating (⊗).

Student's Name _____ Date_____

Teacher's Name _____

Comments _____
_____
_____
_____
_____
_____
_____

Section 9

Turbulence Encountered, Return to Your Seat:

Special Behavior Problems

So by now you have survived not only the first day and the first week of school but maybe even the first month. Now comes the question: What planet did some of these kids in your classroom drop in from? They sure weren't included in any of the discussions in your education classes. And they weren't present during any of your field experiences or student teaching experience. Well, except for maybe Ray and Maria in student teaching. But even they can't hold a candle to these kids! Help! What next?

In this section, we've included some individualized suggestions for managing some of the special behavior problems that seem to make many new teachers the most miserable. The strategies are derived from those we have already discussed in this manual. Take heart. *Even the most difficult problems can be managed*!

Noncompliance

Definition: Not following a direction you give within a reasonable amount of time.

Explanation: Most of the arguing, tantrums, fighting, delaying, or rule breaking are directly connected to avoiding your requests or required tasks. It doesn't matter whether your requests are "to do" something or "to stop" doing something. When you ask a tough kid to do even a simple task (e.g., work on his or her assignment), he or she may argue or throw a tantrum to get you to rescind, withdraw, or back off from your request. Once a teacher withdraws or even modifies the request, then the arguing and "fit throwing" are rewarded.

Coercive interactions with students are the result of following our human tendencies when managing students. This involves excessive prompting, reminding, and arguing, which lead to an *escalation of the problem behavior.* On an average, teachers give 80% plus of their attention to negative student behaviors and a mere 20% or less to positive behaviors. This ratio must be reversed if you hope to minimize inappropriate student behavior and increase appropriate behavior.

Your Immediate Response:

a. When you observe a student *not* doing as you have requested, it is human nature to prompt or nag. Instead, for *minor* instances of noncompliance, first use "Area Praise": Compliment one or two students who are doing as you asked and who are nearby the noncompliant student. For example, you might say, "Jamal, great job of getting to work on your math right away" and "Ling, way to go on your math assignment." If this doesn't prompt your noncompliant student to do as you asked, then you will move on to another strategy, such as a "You *need* to..." request as described in **Section 4**.

What's this Area Praise stuff? I see bad behavior, I jump all over it.

Don't believe Mrs. Muttner!

b. For *major* instances of noncompliance, including those involving yelling, throwing things, ripping up papers, aggression toward others, and the like, Interclass Time Out (ITO) is an appropriate *immediate* response. Once ITO has been completed, your long-term response should include systematic use of positive strategies, such as those described below, for strengthening and reinforcing the student's compliance when it *does* occur.

Your Longer-Term Response:

If you have tried ITO several times, and the same tough kids continue to be noncompliant, it is time to begin using a *systematic strategy* to strengthen and reinforce their direction-following in your classroom. Start your tough noncompliant students on the **Rules Self-Monitoring Program** (described in **Section 8**) for your directions-following rule. Then implement one of the following: **Yes/No Program, Classroom Bingo, Response Cost Lottery**, or the **"Sure I Will" Program**. These programs are outlined in **Section 7**.

Swearing

Definition: Use of words or phrases that are commonly understood to be, or which have been explained to be, unacceptable for use in the classroom or school.

Explanation: Swearing may be used by a student out of anger, for shock value, or even because it has become habitual. Whatever the reason, it is important for students to learn that swearing is unacceptable in many places, including your classroom and school.

Your Immediate Response:

It is not a good idea to ignore swearing in the classroom, hoping it will go away. On the other hand, it is also not a good idea to react as if the student has just committed a felony. A calm, quiet, nonemotional response is called for.

a. A *minor* swearing incident involving an unacceptable word or two, perhaps done quietly but still within your earshot, can be handled discreetly. The first or second time this occurs, a quiet, brief explanation to the student may suffice. You can just say, "Swearing is unacceptable in this classroom. Don't do it again."

The *@!%# kids won't get away with that kind of language in my classroom!

Don't believe Mrs. Muttner!

b. A *major* swearing outburst that disrupts the entire class calls for an immediate Interclass Time Out. You may say, "Your swearing and disruptive behavior are unacceptable in this classroom. You have earned 30 minutes in ITO."

Your Longer-Term Response

If swearing has occurred twice, and you have already tried the suggestion described previously, it is time to begin using a *systematic strategy* to strengthen and reinforce the use of acceptable language in the classroom. Select from the **Home Note**, **Yes/No**, **Classroom Bingo**, or the **Response Cost Lottery** programs. Implement one of them in addition to the short-term responses you are already carrying out.

Disrespectful Behavior

Definition: Verbal or physical behavior toward others, particularly the teacher, that indicates rudeness, contempt, or extreme discourtesy. Disrepect can be expressed in almost endless ways, from a roll of the eyes at something one has said or done, to name calling, references to one's lineage (particularly one's mother!), a certain finger gesture, and the like.

Explanation: Disrespectful behavior may or may not be related to noncompliance. If it is used to get out of doing something the teacher has asked the student to do, it can often be handled successfully by focusing on increasing compliance. If it is not linked to noncompliance, or it is a big enough problem in and of itself, direct intervention is appropriate.

Your Immediate Response

As with swearing, disrespectful behavior should neither be ignored nor overreacted to. A calm, quiet, unemotional response is best.

a. *Minor* and subtle disrespectful behavior may be handled the first time or two with quiet feedback to the student, for example, a private comment such as, "Your eye rolling is unacceptable. Don't do it again." If the behavior occurs again, a *systematic* intervention is needed.

b. *Major* disrespectful behavior that is loud, noticeable, and disruptive of the class may be handled with an ITO. Usually, 20–30 minutes will be sufficient, depending on the age of the student. If the behavior occurs again, a *systematic* intervention may be needed.

> If a kid rolls his eyes at me, his head will roll!

Don't believe Mrs. Muttner!

Your Longer-Term Response

Recurring disrespectful behavior requires a systematic approach for strengthening and reinforcing respectful behavior and weakening or discouraging disrespectful behavior. Again, the **Yes/No**, **Classroom Bingo**, or the **Response Cost Lottery** programs may be used. Follow the instructions given in **Section 7** for the program you select.

Talk-Outs

Definition: Talking or vocalizing without following the classroom rule about speaking. For example, the student simply talks or blurts out without raising her hand, when the classroom rule is "Raise your hand and wait for teacher permission to speak."

Explanation: In addition to being downright annoying and disruptive, "talking-out" can be a tricky problem to tackle. Before trying to solve a classroom talking-out problem, it is essential that you review your classroom talking rule. Does it say what you really want and expect regarding talking behavior? Or does it need a revision? Whether the rule is already acceptable or you need to revise it, you will want to spend some time reteaching it to your class. After you have re-explained it, provide numerous examples and nonexamples of what you want and expect. Model these and have students role-play them. Provide specific feedback to them as they do this.

Consistently follow up and provide positive feedback and reinforcement when students follow your rule and a mild negative consequence when they don't. Do this *every time*, or students will quickly learn that you don't mean business.

Many teachers really don't want students to raise their hands and wait for permission to speak all of the time. These teachers may want hand raising when they are instructing, when there is a classroom discussion, when students are working quietly on assignments at their desks or work stations, etc. It may be all right with these teachers for students to talk quietly with each other when the teacher steps to the doorway to speak briefly with a classroom visitor, when settling in after lunch or recess (particularly before the bell has rung), or when students are working in small groups on collaborative projects. Use the **Red/Green Sign Program** described in **Section 3** to help you handle the different situations for talking.

The point here is that *you* must know what you want and make your rule reflect it. Don't have a hand-raising rule for all situations if that is not what you want and need. You may have a rule such as, "Raise your hand to speak when the red sign is up. When the green sign is up, talk quietly."

Your Immediate Response

First of all, when a student does talk-out (according to your rules), make sure that this behavior doesn't pay off for him or her! For example, if the student blurts out the answer to the question you have just asked, avoid eye contact with him or her (i.e., act as if he or she doesn't even exist), and call on someone else, even if your talker-outer has provided the correct answer. Then reinforce the student you are calling on by saying something like, "Stellajean, thank you for remembering to raise your hand. Your answer is . . . ?"

Your Longer-Term Response

If talking-out is still a chronic problem after you have tried the suggestions discussed above, specifically target talking-out behavior by implementing the **Yes/No**, **Classroom Bingo**, or **Response Cost Lottery** programs. We also strongly recommend that the **Red/Green Sign Program** be a part of your classroom procedures.

Pulling It Together

There is no reason why you cannot use any of the longer-term response strategies mentioned in this section to work on more than one misbehavior at a time. In other words, you can work on decreasing noncompliance and decreasing unacceptable language at the same time, using the same system. For example, if you have selected the **Yes/No Program**, you can award "Yes" tickets for complying with your requests and for using acceptable language. Likewise, "No" tickets can be awarded for not doing as you have requested and for using unacceptable language.

> I was here long before this behavior management stuff, and I'll be here long after it's gone!

Don't believe Mrs. Muttner!

Section 10

Achieving Medallion Status:

Kicking It Up a Notch

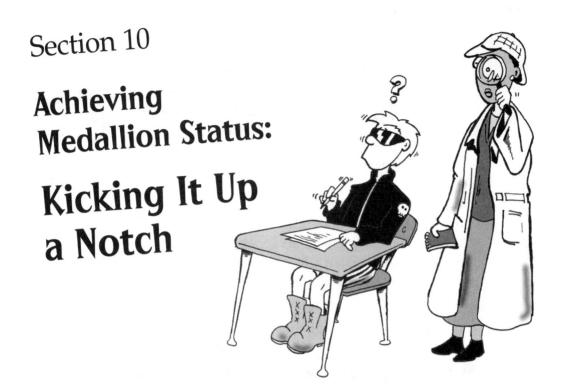

Provide Needed Accommodations:
Leveling the "Playing Field"

Some teachers believe that they must treat all students exactly the same in order to be "fair." Actually, this belief couldn't be more incorrect. Treating all students the same is inherently *unfair*! Students have different strengths, weaknesses, and needs—some with *way* more or less of something than others. In order to be "fair," students' individual differences must be considered.

Nearly every teacher will have a mixture of students in her room who receive special education services or have a physical or mental impairment under Section 504 of the Rehabilitation Act, including having special needs because of a disability, such as attention deficit hyperactivity disorder (ADHD), a hearing or vision impairment, arthritis, an ongoing health problem, obsessive compulsive disorder (OCD), or any of a variety of cognitive disorders.

It is essential that you determine what special requirements the students in your classroom have so that you
can be successful as a teacher. When you have a student
who is experiencing difficulties in your
classroom, talk to his or her parents to
invite their input and to determine any
special needs the student may have.
Many needed accommodations are
very simple and may make all the difference in whether or not the student has
a productive or a wasted school year. A few
common accommodations include:

I treat 'em all the same—like the little animals they are!

Don't believe Mrs. Muttner!

1. Changing student seating (e.g., closer to
    front, closer to teacher, away from dis-
    tractions, surrounded with good role models, etc.).

2. Tailoring homework assignments (e.g., shortened or made simpler).

3. Modifying tests (e.g., verbal instead of written).

4. Supplementing verbal instructions with visual ones (e.g., a written
    list).

5. Repeating and simplifying instructions about in-class and home-
    work assignments.

6. Assigning a classroom peer to serve as a note-taker for the student
    (to copy the peer's notes for the student).

7. Using different instructional materials, pace, or methods.

8. Implementing behavioral/academic contracts.

9. Using supplementary materials designed to accommodate the stu-
    dent's disability.

10. Assigning peer buddies to assist the student with physical tasks that
    the student is incapable of doing (e.g., opening doors, accessing a
    locker, carrying a lunch tray).

11. Providing support and supervision during transitions, disruptions, and field trips.

12. Monitoring stress and fatigue, and adjusting activities appropriately.

13. Establishing a cue between teacher and student (e.g., a signal that means, "I didn't understand it," etc.).

14. Having the student restate or write directions/instructions.

15. Providing the option to stand while working.

16. Providing extra treats and rewards to promote behavior change

17. Providing opportunity for regular physical exercise/activity.

18. Using a tape recorder to record information for the student to review, such as assignments and directions.

19. Communicating frequently with the student's parent(s) (e.g., by phone or by setting up a Home Note Program).

20. Teaching organizational skills (e.g., keeping track of and completing homework assignments).

This list of accommodations is by no means exhaustive. Be a good detective in observing your students and finding out what each one needs in order to be successful. Providing needed accommodations will go a long way in promoting academic success and in *preventing* many behavior problems in your classroom!

Section 11

Using Your Seat Cushion as a Flotation Device:

Some More Tips for Surviving Your First Year

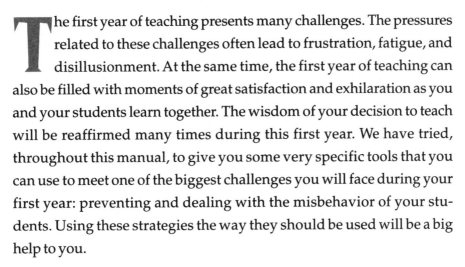

The first year of teaching presents many challenges. The pressures related to these challenges often lead to frustration, fatigue, and disillusionment. At the same time, the first year of teaching can also be filled with moments of great satisfaction and exhilaration as you and your students learn together. The wisdom of your decision to teach will be reaffirmed many times during this first year. We have tried, throughout this manual, to give you some very specific tools that you can use to meet one of the biggest challenges you will face during your first year: preventing and dealing with the misbehavior of your students. Using these strategies the way they should be used will be a big help to you.

You will need more help, however. You will need the time, effort, and energy of a number of your colleagues to help you deal with the frustration and tensions new teachers face. There are a number of strategies you can draw upon, both in and outside your school setting, that can provide assistance.

1. Actively look for and find an ally. Link up with a colleague in your school who shares your approach to teaching and commitment to high standards and who will support you and work together with you to help you become a confident and skilled teacher. This person may be your officially assigned mentor, a fellow first-year teacher, or the experienced teacher down the hall. Someone to share the ups and downs of the year with is critically important.

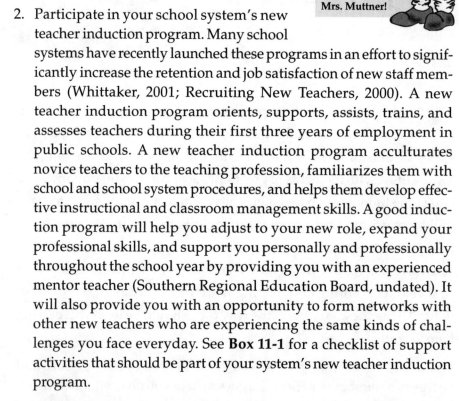

I say let the new teachers sink or swim. Nobody ever did this stuff for me!

Don't believe Mrs. Muttner!

2. Participate in your school system's new teacher induction program. Many school systems have recently launched these programs in an effort to significantly increase the retention and job satisfaction of new staff members (Whittaker, 2001; Recruiting New Teachers, 2000). A new teacher induction program orients, supports, assists, trains, and assesses teachers during their first three years of employment in public schools. A new teacher induction program acculturates novice teachers to the teaching profession, familiarizes them with school and school system procedures, and helps them develop effective instructional and classroom management skills. A good induction program will help you adjust to your new role, expand your professional skills, and support you personally and professionally throughout the school year by providing you with an experienced mentor teacher (Southern Regional Education Board, undated). It will also provide you with an opportunity to form networks with other new teachers who are experiencing the same kinds of challenges you face everyday. See **Box 11-1** for a checklist of support activities that should be part of your system's new teacher induction program.

3. Recruit reinforcement from your school principal. Principals are not widely noted for their high reinforcement rates and/or their enthusiastic support of new teachers, but, hopefully, yours will be. Either

What You Can Expect From a New Teacher "Induction" Program

- Regular (at least weekly) contacts and check-ins with your mentor.

- More in-depth, longer meetings (at least monthly) with your mentor to review issues in detail.

- Opportunities to observe other teachers in their classrooms who do exemplary work so that you can get ideas and see a model teacher in action.

- Opportunities to be observed in your classroom by your mentor on a regular basis to provide you with helpful feedback on your teaching.

- Opportunities to speak with or consult district curriculum specialists. School system curriculum specialists can assist you in learning more about what to teach as well as how and with what instructional methods and materials.

- Encouragement and support.

- More encouragement and support.

way, do not avoid contact with your principal. Involve him or her in your classroom and with your students. Let him or her know that you value his or her interest, advice, and support. Invite him or her to your classroom for special activities with your students. Inviting involvement from your principal is likely to be reciprocated. New teachers who are encouraged and supported by their school administrators, who also make resources within their control available to them, are more likely to have a successful first-year experience.

4. Use effective strategies and document student progress. Teachers who have a higher sense of efficacy, believing that what they do makes a difference, tend to be less vulnerable to job-related stress.

Implementing best practices with your students and carefully monitoring their academic and social performance will make you feel better about the job you are doing with them.

5. Expand your knowledge base. When you feel ready, enroll in a graduate degree program. Also, participate in district- or state-sponsored inservice training. Attend professional conferences (even if they are sometimes on the weekend), read professional journals, surf the Internet, and find examples of research-validated practices and other resources that will help you do a great job. **Box 11-2** lists a number of excellent resources for new teachers to turn to when seeking additional information about a particular concern or problem.

6. Ask for help when you need it. Nobody knows every answer all of the time. However, you can gain a lot of helpful information from other educators.

7. Ventilate every once in awhile. Sometimes the pressures of teaching or the sometimes "odd ways" of the school bureaucracy become so irritating or overwhelming that you may need to let it all hang out. Share your frustrations with a colleague or your mentor. Write a letter describing your frustration and then put it away unsent. Participate in a teacher's chat room on the Internet. Also, refer to **Box 11-3** for a list of additional activities that you should consider to strengthen yourself during your first year on the job.

8. Be positive and kind with your colleagues. Focus on the positive aspects of your job. Try to keep an upbeat attitude about your work. Reinforce your colleagues, and take care of each other.

In the end, you will develop and refine your own personal way of dealing with the challenges and stresses you face as a new teacher. Hopefully, you will find the strategies outlined here beneficial.

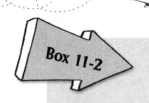

Box 11-2

Recommended Resources for Beginning Teachers

- *Survival Guide for the First-Year Special Education Teacher* (Revised Edition) by Mary Kemper Cohen, Maureen Gale, & Joyce M. Meyer. Council for Exceptional Children, 1994.

- *Teaching Effective Classroom Routines* by Joe Witt, Lynn LaFleur, Gale Naquin, & Donna Gilbertson. Sopris West, 1999.

- *The First Days of School: How to Be an Effective Teacher* by Harry K. Wong & Rosemary T. Wong. Harry K. Wong Publications, 1998.

- *Don't Shoot the Dog! The New Art of Teaching and Training* (Revised Edition) by Karen Pryor. Bantam Books, 1999.

- *Teacher's Little Book of Wisdom* by Bob Algozzine. ICS Books, 1995.

- *50 Simple Ways to Make Teaching More Fun* by Bob Algozzine. Sopris West, 1993.

- *Get 'Em on Task: A Computer Signaling Program to Teach Attending and Self-Management Skills* by Brad Althouse, William Jenson, Marilyn Likins, & Daniel Morgan. Sopris West, 2000.

- *The Tough Kid Book: Practical Classroom Management Strategies* by Ginger Rhode, William R. Jenson, & H. Kenton Reavis. Sopris West, 1993.

- *The Tough Kid Tool Box* by William R. Jenson, Ginger Rhode, & H. Kenton Reavis. Sopris West, 1994.

- *The Teacher's Encyclopedia of Behavior Management* by Randy Sprick. Sopris West, 1995.

- *Strategies and Tactics for Effective Instruction* (Second Edition) by Bob Algozzine, Jim Ysseldyke, & Judy Elliott. Sopris West, 1997.

- *The New Teacher's Survival Guide: Stuff that Works* by Kathleen McConnell Fad & James E. Gilliam. Sopris West, 2000.

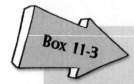

Box 11-3

Some Stress Busters for New Teachers

- Exercise regularly. It revives, energizes, and relaxes you.

- Take a yoga class.

- Get plenty of rest and sleep. Problems and frustrations are not as formidable when you are rested.

- Don't schedule all of your time. Leave some "nothing planned" time in your planner.

- Don't procrastinate. When something is continuously hanging over you, it drains your energy and creates tension.

- Pursue a hobby or learn a new skill totally unrelated to your teaching job. Concentrating on enjoying an activity that is completely different will help you forget about school for a while.

- Keep your sense of humor!

Section 12

Become a Top Gun:

Secrets of Master Teachers

Without a doubt, one of the most difficult challenges faced by new teachers is managing the behavior of their students, both individually and as a group. "Help! These kids are driving me crazy!" is often heard from first-year teachers. The techniques and strategies presented throughout this book are research-based interventions that, when implemented as directed, will help you achieve more success and gain greater satisfaction during your first year of teaching. Not only will these techniques help you, they will help your students achieve more academically, behaviorally, and socially.

Underlying the use of these powerful strategies is a common set of teaching skills that are invariably observed in the classrooms of the most effective teachers. These skills are briefly described on the next few pages:

1. **Effective teachers know that the best way to deal with serious behavior problems is to prevent them from occurring in the first place.** Student behavior problems are inevitable. They go with the

territory. When the behavior problems of individual students or an entire classroom mushroom and escalate, even the best teachers have great difficulty dealing effectively with these kinds of situations. While there are effective strategies that teachers and other school personnel can use to deal with behavioral crisis situations, they are not the primary focus of this manual.

Instead, we have concentrated your attention on universal prevention strategies. These are strategies that have proven to be effective in preventing serious behavior problems and in promoting appropriate achievement-oriented behavior in all students (Kerr & Nelson, 1998). The idea is to learn how to design positive, structured, educational environments that emphasize high expectations, actively teaching students in ways that promote success, and providing opportunities for students to learn appropriate, alternative ways of behaving in difficult situations.

2. **Effective teachers accentuate the positive and eliminate (or drastically curtail) the negative.** Perhaps the simplest and most direct technique a teacher can use to effectively manage student behavior is to "catch 'em being good" (Sugai & Horner, 1999). This technique may also be one of the more difficult techniques for new teachers (and experienced teachers) to use, because the systematic use of positive reinforcement just doesn't seem to be a naturally occurring adult behavior in our schools. Most teachers and other school personnel tend to fall back on their natural tendency to notice only when inappropriate behavior occurs, unless they have been taught to do otherwise. Nagging, reprimanding, and criticizing are, it seems, a popular way of dealing with student behavior, since we see these kinds of negative behavior management techniques used frequently in schools. While they may be effective

> *Effective teachers accentuate the positive and eliminate (or drastically curtail) the negative.*

in temporarily suppressing inappropriate behavior, they are virtually useless in teaching students how to behave appropriately over the long term.

When students receive positive recognition and reinforcement for behaving like a student (in the best sense of the word), they tend to behave that way more often in the future (Alberto & Troutman, 1999). For virtually all of your students, including the toughest kid in your classroom, your approval and your attention are valuable resources. When you praise your students' efforts and accomplishments, you are providing the kind of attention that promotes learning and achievement. *The catch is that you need to be positively reinforcing much more often than you might think is necessary.* You must also significantly curtail your use of negative attention (e.g., "Don't do that!"; "Stop it!"; "Sit down and be quiet!").

The general rule is that your use of positives should be *a minimum of four times greater* than your use of negatives (in other words, a 4:1 ratio of positives to negatives.) This means that for each time you nag, criticize, or reprimand, you need to catch your students being good four times (Latham, 1997). As with any new way of behaving (and being mostly positive is a new way of behaving for many of us), proficiency requires concentration and practice. The benefits of becoming a proficient praiser are huge and very much worth your time and effort. **Nothing else you do will work if your classroom is not much more positive than it is negative!**

3. **Effective teachers view behavior management problems as instructional problems.** When behavior problems occur with either individual students or an entire classroom, one of the first questions often asked is, "What is wrong with this student(s)?" Instead of asking that question, try asking these questions instead: What is wrong with my instructional program? Are there specific things going on or

absent from the program that may be encouraging or triggering this inappropriate behavior? Is the lesson or learning task too long, too difficult, or too boring? Does the student have the prerequisite skills needed to successfully complete the task? Are the assignment directions clear? Does the student know the expectations for this assignment? Asking these kinds of questions *first* will probably give you answers that will tell you what to change in your instructional program to promote learning and to avoid serious behavior problems both now and later on (Kauffman et al., 2002).

4. **Effective teachers know that "telling is *not* teaching."** Good teaching is very *active* for both students and teachers. Demonstrating, practicing, providing feedback, and more practicing is how good teachers teach (Algozzine & Kay, 2002). John Wooden, the legendary UCLA basketball coach, once said this about his approach to coaching and teaching: "To make sure the goal is achieved, I created eight laws of learning: explanation, demonstration, imitation, repetition, repetition, repetition, repetition, and repetition." Coach Wooden led his UCLA basketball teams to ten NCAA national championships during his coaching career.

> " *Good teaching is very* **active** *for both students and teachers.* "

Telling a student to "behave appropriately" is almost certain to fail as a strategy. *Teaching* a student to "behave appropriately" is almost a sure bet to succeed. If you want your students to behave *responsibly*, you will need to take responsibility for teaching them how.

5. **Effective teachers know what is going on in their classrooms.** This might seem very, very obvious. However, keeping track of student behavior in a systematic way is a skill that requires concentration and practice. This skill has sometimes been referred to as "with-it-ness," and it has been identified as a very important characteristic of effective teachers (Kounin, 1970):

- *With-it-ness* is the ability to know how to anticipate problems before they become problems and to be able to nip them in the bud.

- *With-it-ness* is knowing that a problem is brewing in the early, early stages.

- *With-it-ness* is having "eyes in the back of your head."

- *With-it-ness* enables you to anticipate where problems might occur and to act quickly to maintain an orderly and productive learning environment. In other words, you need to learn how to walk, talk, look, listen, and teach at the same time if you want to be "with it."

6. **Effective teachers recognize that the *only* behavior they can directly control is their *own* behavior.** Behavior management is often viewed as a *control* issue. You can almost hear your principal asking you after your first week of school, "Who is in control—you or your students?" These kinds of questions may lead you to increase pressure on yourself to attempt to control your students' behavior through the use of reprimands and punishment.

   Trying to *control* your students is focusing on the wrong problem. You need to change your way of looking at control issues by adhering to the following basic rules:

   - You can't directly control your students.

   - The only individual in your classroom whose behavior you can control is your own.

   - If you want to change your students' behavior for the better, you will need to change your behavior first.

   All of the strategies and techniques presented in this kit describe ways you can change your behavior so that your students' behavior will improve. Using these techniques in the manner described will be the best way to make improvements happen.

7. **Effective teachers teach relentlessly.** "Relentless" teaching is probably the most effective method of preventing and dealing with behavior problems available to all teachers, new and experienced alike.

   What do we mean by relentless teaching? Relentless teaching means what it says. It means demonstrating concepts and skills, providing practice opportunities, providing positive feedback, providing corrective feedback as needed, catching your students being good, making accommodations, tracking progress, monitoring performance and behavior, and making changes based on student behavior, consistently and predictably. Relentless teaching means that when you are in doubt about what to do or how to deal with a problem, you teach. You teach up a storm. *You become a relentless teacher.*

8. **Effective teachers know how to keep the dishes spinning.** A good teacher is a bit like the juggler who places dishes on top of a line of tall poles and spins them all at once, running back and forth along the line to make sure that none of the dishes fall off and break.

To succeed, our dish-spinning juggler must be quick to respond when he sees a wobbly dish requiring attention. He must recognize and deftly move down the row of poles to make the necessary adjustments. He must be very, very alert.

And, if a dish happens to drop to the floor, he simply replaces it with a new dish and starts it spinning anew with the same level of enthusiasm and determination.

We hope you see the similarities between the dish spinner and an effective teacher. Alert. Active. Quick to respond at the earliest sign of difficulty. Able to make the necessary adjustments to improve performance. Undeterred by temporary setbacks. Relentless. Confident.

Secrets of Master Teachers Summary

Master teachers:

- Understand that the best way to deal with serious behavior problems is to prevent them from occurring in the first place.

- Accent the positive and eliminate (or drastically curtail) the negative.

- View behavioral problems as instructional problems.

- Remember that telling is not teaching.

- Know what is going on in their classroom.

- Recognize that the only behavior they can truly control is their own.

- Teach relentlessly.

- Keep the dishes spinning.

We urge you to read these pages more than once. Read them over and over and over again. Commit this list of effective teaching behaviors to memory. You will use them year in and year out, not only during your first year as a teacher. Your teaching style will benefit, and your students will enjoy learning—the goal of every new teacher!

Happy landing!

References

Alberto, P. A., & Troutman, A. C. (1999). *Applied behavior analysis for teachers* (5th ed.). Columbus, OH: Merrill.

Algozzine, B., & Kay, P. (2002). Promising practices for preventing problem behaviors. In B. Algozzine & P. Kay (Eds.), *Preventing problem behaviors: A handbook of successful prevention strategies.* Thousand Oaks, CA: Corwin Press.

Emmer, E. T., Evertson, C. M., Clements, B. S., & Worsham, M. E. (1997). *Classroom management for secondary teachers* (4th ed.). Boston: Allyn and Bacon.

Evertson, C. M., Emmer, E. T., Clements, B. S., & Worsham, M. E. (1997). *Classroom management for elementary teachers* (4th ed.). Boston: Allyn and Bacon.

Forehand, R. (1977). Child noncompliance to parental requests: Behavior analysis and treatment. In M. Hersen, R. M. Eisler, & P. M. Miller (Eds.), *Progress in behavior modification* (Vol. 5) (pp. 111–148). New York: Academic Press.

Gersten, R., Keating, T., Yovanoff, P., & Harniss, M. K. (2001). Working in special education: Factors that enhance special educators' intent to stay. *Exceptional Children, 67,* 549–567.

Hamlet, C. C., Axelrod, S., & Kuerschner, S. (1984). Eye contact as an antecedent to compliant behavior. *Journal of Applied Behavior Analysis, 17,* 553–557.

Harris & Associates, Inc. (1991). *The Metropolitan Life survey of American teachers, 1991: The first year: New teachers' expectations and ideals.* New York: Metropolitan Life Insurance Company.

Hequet, M. (1990). Non-sales incentive programs inspire service heroes. *Reward and Recognition, 8,* 3–17.

Jenson, W. R., Rhode, G., & Reavis, H. K. (1994). *The tough kid tool box.* Longmont, CO: Sopris West.

Jesse, V. C. (1990). *Compliance training and generalization effects using a compliance matrix and spinner system.* Unpublished dissertation, University of Utah, Salt Lake City, UT.

Johnson, S. M., & Birkeland, S. E. (2002). *Pursuing a "sense of success": New teachers explain their career decisions.* Paper presented at Annual Meeting of the American Educational Research Association, New Orleans, LA, April 1–5, 2002.

Jones, F. H. (2000). *Tools for teaching.* Santa Cruz, CA: Fredric H. Jones & Associates.

Kauffman, J. M., Mostert, M. P., Trent, S. C., & Hallahan, D. P. (2002). *Managing classroom behavior: A reflective case-based approach* (3rd ed.). Boston: Allyn and Bacon.

Kerr, M. M., & Nelson, C. M. (1998). *Strategies for managing behavior problems in the classroom* (3rd ed.). Columbus, OH: Merrill.

Kounin, J. (1970). *Discipline and group management in classrooms.* New York: Holt, Rinehart, and Winston.

Latham, G. (1997). *Behind the schoolhouse door: Eight skills every teacher should have.* Logan, UT: Mountain Plains Regional Resource Center, Utah State University.

Martin-LeMaster, J. (1990). *Increasing classroom compliance of noncompliant elementary age students.* Unpublished dissertation, University of Utah, Salt Lake City, UT.

Mayer, G. (1995). Preventing antisocial behavior in the schools. *Journal of Applied Behavior Analysis, 28,* 467–478.

Moran, C., Stobbe, J., Baron, W., Miller, J., & Moir, E. (2000). *Keys to the classroom: A teacher's guide to the first month of school.* (2nd ed.). Thousand Oaks, CA: Corwin Press.

Paine, S. C., Radicchi, J., Rosellini, L. C., Deutchman, L., & Darch, C. B. (1983). *Structuring your classroom for academic success.* Champaign, IL: Research Press.

Patterson, G. R. (1982). *Coercive family process*. Eugene, OR: Castilia Publishing.

Proctor, M. A., & Morgan, D. (1991). Effectiveness of a response cost raffle procedure on the disruptive classroom behavior of adolescents with behavior problems. *School Psychology Review, 20*, 97–109.

Recruiting New Teachers. (1999). *A guide to developing teacher induction programs*. Belmont, MA: Recruiting New Teachers, Inc.

Recruiting New Teachers. (2000). *Learning the ropes: Urban teacher induction programs and practices in the United States*. Belmont, MA: Recruiting New Teachers, Inc.

Rhode, G., Jenson, W. R., & Reavis, H. K. (1992). *The tough kid book: Practical classroom management strategies*. Longmont, CO: Sopris West.

School Renaissance Institute (2000). *44 routines that make a difference: Strategies for the effective classroom*. Madison, WI: School Renaissance Institute, Inc.

Southern Regional Educational Board. (Undated). *Reduce your losses: Help new teachers become veteran teachers*. Atlanta, GA: Southern Regional Educational Board.

Sugai, G., & Horner, R. H. (1999). Discipline and behavioral support: Practices, pitfalls, and promises. *Effective School Practices, 17*, 10–22.

Van Houten, R., & Doleys, D. (1983). Are social reprimands effective? In S. Axelrod and J. Apsche (Eds.), *The effects of punishment on human behavior* (pp. 45–70). New York: Academic Press.

Whitaker, S. D. (2001). Supporting beginning special education teachers. *Focus on Exceptional Children, 34*(4), 1–18.

Witt, J., LaFleur, L., Naquin, G., & Gilbertson, D. (1999). *Teaching effective classroom routines*. Longmont, CO: Sopris West.

Witt, J. C., & Elliot, S. N. (1982). The response cost lottery: A time efficient and effective classroom intervention. *Journal of School Psychology, 20*, 155–161.

Wong, H. K., & Wong, R. T. (1998). *How to be an effective teacher: The first days of school*. Mountain View, CA: Harry K. Wong Publications.

Other Publications of Interest

The Tough Kid Book: Practical Classroom Management Strategies

Ginger Rhode PhD, William R. Jenson PhD, and H. Kenton Reavis EdD

When a student's aggression, tantrums, noncompliance, and poor academic performance thwart progress in your classroom and discourage you as a teacher, it's time to get help! *The Tough Kid Book* offers creative techniques that are effective and can be implemented without costly materials or a big time investment. Clearly in tune with today's children, the authors of this well-timed publication are realistic in their approach and successful in their effort to provide helpful solutions to today's educators. (2C40TK)

The Tough Kid Tool Box

William R. Jenson PhD, Ginger Rhode PhD, and H. Kenton Reavis EdD

Created to both complement and supplement *The Tough Kid Book*, the Tool Box provides additional and more in-depth explanations and strategies. Each of the book's seven sections begins with a definition, a description, and steps to accomplish a specific intervention. Troubleshooting tips are offered in every chapter, as are "making-it-even-better" ideas that show you how to improvise or enhance an intervention. Most helpful, however, are the "tools" themselves—reproducible, timesaving forms, such as Home Notes, Mystery Motivators, Bingo Cards, and many more. (2C58TB)

The Tough Kid Social Skills Book

Susan M. Sheridan PhD

When students don't know how to resolve conflict, express frustration, or interact with others, they have difficulty with schoolwork and in their personal lives. This *Tough Kid* component addresses ten specific social skills, such as recognizing and expressing feelings, using self-control, solving arguments, and joining in. Decide today to improve the quality of your classroom and a student's chance to succeed in life. *The Tough Kid Social Skills Book* is a great place to start! Includes reproducibles. (2C75SOCIAL)

The Tough Kid Video Series

Eight of the most prominent education experts offer practical strategies to help you turn your "tough kids" into achieving kids! The six-video set includes: *Behavior Management: Positive Approaches* (Bill Jenson); *Behavior Management: Reductive Techniques* (Ken Reavis and Ginger Rhode); *Social Skills* (Hill Walker); *Instructional Strategies* (Jim Ysseldyke and Bob Algozzine); *Study Skills* (Anita Archer); and *Schoolwide Techniques* (Randy Sprick).

Includes a 222-page manual for staff development use, reproducibles, and one copy of *The Tough Kid Book*. Each video is 50 minutes. (2C76SERIES: Series; 2C76RENT: 8-Week Rental; Videos can be purchased individually for $500.00 each; please call.)

The Tough Kid Audio Series

H. Kenton Reavis EdD, Ginger Rhode PhD, and William R. Jenson PhD

This comprehensive audio series will help you better teach, work with, and positively influence "tough kids." The two-level Series (basic and advanced) includes these titles:

- Tough Kids Are Our Strongest Weakness: Do's and Don'ts of Successful Schools
- Closer and Quieter vs. Further and Louder
- Positives: The Heart of an Effective Classroom for Tough Kids
- Additional Positive Stuff That Works
- The Fair Pair: Social Skills and Teaching Appropriate Behavior
- Homenotes
- Advertising for Success and Self-Monitoring Programs
- Lessons Learned